When The Word Meets The Wallet:

The Financial Bible

Maurice E. Miller Jr.

CERTIFIED FINANCIAL PLANNER™

Editor: Tenita C. Johnson

Cover Design: Erica Mozee

Maurice E Miller Jr

Copyright © 2018, 2024 Maurice E. Miller Jr.
All rights reserved. This book or any portion thereof
may not be reproduced or used in any manner whatsoever
without the express written permission of the publisher
except for the use of brief quotations in a book review.

Scripture quotations are from the Holy Bible, English Standard Version, copyright © 2001, 2007, 2011, 2016 by Crossway Bibles, a division of Good News Publishers. Used by permission. All rights reserved.

The information contained herein is not intended to be a source of advice with respect to the material presented, and the information and/or documents contained in this publication do not constitute investment advice. The ideas and strategies should never be used without first assessing your own personal and financial situation, or without consulting a financial professional.

ISBN: 1-7329110-0-2
ISBN-13: 978-1-7329110-0-0

DEDICATION

I thank my father, Maurice E. Miller, Sr., for introducing me to God and hard work. I thank God everyday that he blessed me with such a loving and caring father. You are missed, but your memory lives on in all of us. This book is dedicated to you.

Table of Contents

ACKNOWLEDGMENTS	1
Preface	2
1 Introduction	4
2 Foundation	8
3 Brick I: Generating Income	18
4 Brick II: Planning	23
5 Brick III: Creating Money Systems	28
6 Brick IV: Wise Counsel	37
7 Brick V: Saving	41
8 Brick VI: Giving	49
9 Spiritual Reasons to Invest	59
10 Practical Reasons to Invest	73
11 Investment Options	84
Bank Instruments	85
Money Market Accounts	86
CDs	87
Bonds	91
Annuities	98
Stocks	109
Mutual Funds	114
Exchange-Traded Funds	123
12 Life Insurance Planning	126
13 Educational Planning	144
14 Retirement Planning	153
15 Asset Protection	191
16 Estate Planning	201
17 Wealth Killers	215

Closing Remarks	229
Resource Page	232
ABOUT THE AUTHOR	233

ACKNOWLEDGMENTS

To my beautiful wife, Laneetra: Thank you for being a constant in my life. You're a constant source of love and encouragement, and you're a great example of a godly wife and mother. I pray you will continue to enjoy the fruit of your labor. I pray God blesses you for your faithfulness to Him and our family.

To our five disciples, Jordyn, Josiah, Justus, Gabriella & Joy: You all are the greatest children a father could ask for. Your brilliance, wit, sense of humor, and love for God amazes me.

To my mom: I never appreciated all that you are until recently. Your soft, peaceful spirit is something that blesses everyone, and I appreciate all you've done for me. Thank you for your patience with me throughout my life.

To my sister, Najah: Thank you for being a great example of a sister and helping me understand the value of working and getting an education. Thank you for your support and for always being there to bail me out when I made bad decisions.

To my brother, William: I know I don't express it enough, but I do love you and appreciate you.

To my cousins, aunts and uncles: Thank you from the bottom of my heart for always being there to support me. For most of my life, I felt like I had multiple parents because you all were there every step of the way. You have always treated me like a son.

Thank you to my good friend and business partner, Arti Batra Esquire, for assisting with the estate planning portion of this book.

Preface

While I've been fortunate enough to overcome many of the challenging circumstances in which I was born into, financial management wasn't taught in my home. Thus, I've made many financial mistakes along the way. By the grace of God, I've been able to overcome them and share what I've learned over my career, which spans nearly two decades. This book was birthed out of many personal mistakes, failures, hard times and, eventually, triumphs.

Throughout my career, I've worked in the Metro Detroit area with people from various worldviews. While some of these worldviews overlap as it relates to money management, I've found that the Christian community seemed to have the least amount of understanding. As I grew in my career and faith, this became problematic for me. A significant amount of Scripture directly speaks to money management or indirectly applies to money. Even though the Bible serves as a guide, it is often misunderstood or misinterpreted, or some people simply aren't reading it at all. Financial management touches nearly everything and everyone. While it can appear to be difficult to understand, the Bible is specific about money if we read it closely.

Whether it was someone telling me that investing was a form of greed, or someone telling me that the Bible prohibits the very things I was advising clients to do, I was forced to reconsider if my theology surrounding money was wrong. What I found was overwhelmingly positive and apparent that God has much to say about how we manage our money. I also found a need for a grounded voice in financial management from a Christian viewpoint. By no means am I any type of biblical scholar, but I can bring a unique perspective to the conversation.

There seems to be two extremes in the world of financial management for Christians. On one hand, you may have someone who is well-versed in

Scripture, yet lacks practical financial discipline. On the other hand, you may have someone who's an experienced financial advisor, and can educate you on investing, but can't tell you why God would want you to invest. I'm not minimizing either side because they both are important. However, I am suggesting that it is vital for Christians to have a foundation of both sides. Or else, we'll be ill- equipped to make proper decisions. Much of what I find in the Christian community masking itself as financial advice is often a worldly perspective of wealth and success. My mission is to be a voice of reason, explanation, and application of God's word as it relates to finances.

We must use the same amount of diligence when it comes to money management as we do other trivial things that have little to no impact on our lives. This book has been years in the making. My life and personal experiences as a Christian, a man, a husband, a father and a financial advisor are all wrapped in this text. My hope is to give a Biblical step-by-step guide to managing money. However, this book speaks from the vantage point of someone who works in the financial industry. This is the voice I believe is lacking.

Throughout this text, we will reference many Scriptures. Some will be spelled out, while others will be referenced for you to read later. My goal is not to preach to you, but to show you that everything I put in this book is heavily and heavenly rooted in Scripture. This is not just another book about God, money or both. This is your handbook on how to build, manage and share the wealth God gives us all the ability to create. You will be challenged and sometimes, downright upset. But remember, it's all rooted in Scripture. Before you read any further, grab a pen, notepad and a highlighter to take good notes. My sheer hope and belief is that if you apply what you read, you will be an even greater blessing to your family, community, church and, most importantly, God. Read, understand and apply!

1 Introduction

Many publications set an expectation for what you'll learn throughout the book, and I will definitely get to that. But I also want to start with a simple line that I'm sure you've heard before: "Nothing in life is risk-free." This statement is typically spoken concerning sales pitches for investments or "stepping out on faith." However, I want you to look at it for what it's worth, without bringing anything else into the picture.

Though some things may have little or minimum risk, *everything* carries some type of risk. I'm not trying to convince you to do anything, other than realize that your life can't be bound by fear. There's nothing to be gained if you don't take risks. Risk is simply defined by the chance that something unfavorable could happen. You could go to work, expecting to work 40 hours, only to work 30 because of a low workload. You could get into a car accident backing out of your driveway or leaving the grocery store. Plain and simple, nothing is risk-free.

What You Won't Get From This Book

Any time the subject of money comes up, most people's suspicion antennae go up, and rightfully so. We're in an age where everyone is an expert. Everyone has something to sell. Most of us are presented with a thousand offers a day. This is also an age of deception, where we've seen Ponzi schemes left and right, leaving the public in an uproar and sometimes overly cynical with anyone who brings up the subject. I want to highlight a few things that you will not get from this book.

Get-Rich-Quick Scheme

Nothing in this book will help you get rich or gain wealth overnight. As you'll see throughout this book and, more importantly, *The Good Book*, becoming wealthy is something that can happen over time, but most times, not overnight.

Name It & Claim It

I'm not picking on any central belief system, but nothing that I will teach you will work by just reading it—or even praying about it. There are going to be many areas of application. If you're not willing to put in the work, there's a 0% chance of a success rate. While I can't guarantee you 100% success with anything, what I can guarantee is that if you believe just speaking words with no action behind them will lead to a fruitful financial future, there's a 100% chance of failure. Anyone who tells you that you can make poor financial decisions, and yet reap a reward, is frankly setting you up to fail.

Prosperity Message

Throughout this book, you will see terms like *rich* and *wealth*. While those terms are often used in the Bible, I use those terms in the context in which they are written. I never want to give the impression that we will all be rich or wealthy, by any stretch of the imagination. Some of us won't be, but that doesn't mean we won't experience a good and fruitful life As we'll see throughout this book and Scripture, God is much more concerned about us being faithful to Him than He is with making sure we are financially well-off. Some will access that level of financial well-being, but not everyone.

Non-Biblical Stances

As I started writing this book, I made a mistake that many of us make as we prepare to read Scripture. I had my format and framework for how I wanted everything to go. I dug deep into the Bible to find Scriptures that supported the positions I wanted to take. The shortfall with this is the conflict that takes place when you take an approach that's not supported by the Bible. My promise to you is to not present anything that isn't rooted in the Word of God.

What You Will Gain

This book is great for you if you want to know more about God's purpose for money. This is a great resource to gain clear application from Scripture that directly and indirectly relates to money. You'll also receive action steps to either get you on track, keep you on track, or place you on a better track. Throughout my career, I've learned people better understand content and context when given examples. So, we'll also look at some real-life examples. You'll also receive real-life resources. Everything in this book may not apply to you, but some parts surely will. Make sure you read it from cover to cover and read it multiple times.

In particular, we'll cover what God has to say about:
- The Biblical Purpose for Money & Wealth
- How to Honor God Financially
- Savings
- Trusting in Wealth & Riches
- Building a Legacy
- Financial Wisdom
- Giving
- Planning
- Investing
- Retirement Planning
- Educational Planning
- Insurance Planning
- Estate Planning
- God's Expectations Concerning These Areas

SECTION I
Building The House

2   Foundation

As we begin to take this journey on Biblical wealth management, I want you to begin to imagine a house being built from the ground up. You have the blueprints in your hand that shows you exactly what needs to go into this house to complete it. The foundation of this Biblical wealth management house is the Bible. Once we lay a strong foundation, we can begin to build a strong house brick by brick. Once the bricks are laid we will begin to fill the rooms and complete the house. This is the framework of how everything will be laid out.

Before we can truly build on what God has to say about money, let's first look at the godly purpose behind money. Stand up and say this as loud as you can: "Money is good!" Say it again. "Money is good!" Be honest. That probably made you feel pretty uncomfortable, and I can understand why. For most of our lives, we've been erroneously taught that money is a bad thing or, as we like to say in the church, "Money is the root of all evil." One must consider that if God created it, is it really bad, or is the problem with the person instead of the money? Money can't do anything but be money. So, let's go to the Scriptures and see what the real problem is. In the Bible, 1 Timothy 6:10 says, *For the **love** of money is a root of **all kinds** of evils. It is through this craving that some have wandered away from the faith and pierced themselves with many pangs.*

Did you notice how a few words changes everything? The obsession of money is the problem, not the possession of money. The Scripture tells us that if we fall into the trap of loving money, it becomes the root of all kinds of evil, but not every evil in life. Meaning, not all evils in life are related to money, but the love of money often leads to different forms of evils. If we were able to poll individuals who committed adultery, I'm confident the cause in most cases would not be related to money. On the other hand, the love of money often leads people to lie, steal, and kill.

Money is a necessary part of our survival, as individuals and communities. Even non-profit companies need money to operate. Otherwise, whatever mission they pursue won't happen. No matter what you desire to do in life or ministry, there's a dollar amount behind it. Without the finances to back the mission, you'll be hard pressed to get it done. As my good friend Ian Watts says, "No money, no mission." God knows exactly what our needs and desires are, and the financial number we need to meet those needs. Ecclesiastes 10:19 says, *Bread is made for laughter, and wine gladdens life, and money answers everything.* This Scripture doesn't mean that money will solve every problem we face. However, it does suggest that, no matter what we want to do, there's going to be some sort of financial need behind it. Whether it's feeding the homeless, building homes or reaching foreign countries with the gospel, you need money to do it.

For us to truly appreciate these passages of Scripture, we must keep things in proper perspective. From the onset, I wanted to make it clear that my goal is not to tell you that God wants you to be rich. Instead, my goal is to show you how to apply the Scriptures with wisdom because wisdom is what we need above all things. Not to pick on non-profits, but if you look at many of them who seek to end hunger, homelessness or even cancer, we don't lack resources for these causes. There are millions, if not billions of resources for these good causes, yet the problems don't seem to ever go away.

From the Christian standpoint, we must realize that money has its purpose in God's plan. It does not replace God. Money can only go so far. Proverbs 3:13-16 says, *Blessed is the one who finds wisdom, and the one who gets understanding, for the gain from her is better than gain from silver and her profit better than gold. She is more precious than jewels, and nothing you desire can compare with her. Long life is in her right hand; in her left hand are riches and honor.* Money without wisdom will only increase many of the current world problems we're dealing with, both personally and globally. It's funny how we often criticize our government for doing the very things we do financially. We often complain about the national budget and the deficit. Yet, we have very little opposition to our individual overspending. If we can agree money is good, and it is indeed a godly thing, one must ask, "What's the purpose of money?"

God's Purpose for Money

While I believe we all can find various reasons for money, I believe the Bible shows us four primary reasons for having money.

1. To confirm God's covenant he made with his chosen people (Deutoronomy 8:18)
2. To do good in the earth (1 Timothy 6:17-19)
3. For our enjoyment (Ecclesiastes 15:18-19)
4. To leave an inheritance (Proverbs 13:22)

Confirming God's Covenant

Since we've begun to uproot some of the bad theology that relates to money, it's just as important that we fill those holes. Deuteronomy 8:18 says, *You shall remember the Lord your God, for it is he who gives you power to get wealth, that he may confirm his covenant that he swore to your fathers, as it is this day.* God's purpose for money is to confirm His covenant that He promised to Abraham in Genesis 17. God promised him that he would be the father of many nations, and those nations would multiply and be fruitful. That's what we're supposed to use money to accomplish. We are to use money to advance God's kingdom and bless others.

What type of God would create a people, tell them He cares about them, but doesn't make provision for them? Each time God gives us the ability to make money, He is constantly reminding us that it is He who gives us these abilities and that He has a plan for His people. Notice in the Scripture, which was written thousands of years ago, that it says, *…that he swore to your fathers as it is this day*. That day spills into today. There's a much bigger purpose at hand than what we often realize. Money is just a tool that God has given us to further His purpose here on earth. So, if God's intention in giving us money is to confirm His covenant, then we must take an honest look in the mirror. Are we using the resources God has given us to confirm and further our covenant with Him?

To do good in the earth

As God has given us money, he also reminds us that the money is not for our purposes, but His, which includes caring for those in need. We see in the 15th chapter of Deutoronmy, Moses giving orders that the children of Israel were to willingly share, both lending and giving freely as their brothers were in need. The chapter goes as far as to challenge them not to delay helping because they may be close to the 7th year, which was the year of release where debts were to be forgiven.

In I Timothy 5 The Apostle Paul mentions the person who is worse than an unbeliever and denied the faith is the person who won't provide support for their relatives, especially for the members of his household. Though he was providing instruction for caring for widows, who seemed to be putting a strain on the local church financially because their family wouldn't take care of them, the point is God also gives us money to provide for our families.

We also see in 1 Timothy 6:17-19 the Apostle Paul wrote, *"As for the rich in this present age, charge them not to be haughty, nor to set their hopes on the uncertainty of riches, but on God, who richly provides us with everything to enjoy. They are to do good, to be rich in good works, to be generous and ready to share, thus storing up treasure for themselves as a good foundation for the future, so that they may take hold of that which is truly life."* Lets remember Paul was writing to Timothy, his disciple, giving him instructions on how his church should function, which means Paul was talking to followers of Jesus, who were rich.

Our Enjoyment

Solomon wrote in Ecclesiastes 5:18-19, *"Behold, what I have seen to be good and fitting is to eat and drink and find enjoyment in all the toil with which one toils under the sun the few days of his life that God has given him, for this is his lot. Everyone also to whom God has given wealth and possessions and power to enjoy them, and to accept his lot and rejoice in his toil—this is the gift of God."* Work is a blessing, and what comes from that work is also a blessing from God. It's OK to enjoy some of what God has given us financially, as long as we don't begin to live solely for greed filled desires, which is what Solomon is warning against and calls vanity.

Leaving an Inheritance

Lastly, God gives us money to leave an inheritance to our children's children. We will touch on this more, but God is expecting us to leave our future generations more than just our thoughts, or morals. Proverbs 13:22 admonishes us to make sure our future generations aren't starting from zero.

How Can We Honor God Financially?

If the purpose behind God doing anything is to confirm a covenant, then we as His people must do our part. As with any covenant, there are multiple parties involved. The covenant works best when all parties understand their roles and are faithful to those roles. If you consider marriage, which is one of God's greatest covenants, it indeed involves three parties (husband, wife and God). All parties have a role to play in the marriage. The beauty and strength of that covenant is going to be based on the faithfulness of each party.

When we look at our world financially, I think we can all agree that the issue never has been whether God has been faithful to us, but whether or not we have been faithful to God. As we've advanced technologically, we see even greater opportunities to access information, launch businesses and create innovation, which often leads to greater money-making opportunities. Yet, one could argue that the financial landscape across the world is actually getting worse. If we examine the area that I live, work and worship in, we see polarizing realities of what happens when people are not financially faithful to God's instructions.

Honoring God financially starts internally. As we see in Matthew regarding the parable of the sower, many of us have verbally said we wanted to "do better" financially. But the seed of "doing better" fell on shallow ground and never took root outside of our momentary excitement. Honoring God financially starts and ends with a firm understanding of what the Bible says about how to do such a thing. Proverbs 3:9 is a great starting point: *Honor the Lord with your wealth and with the first fruits of all your produce.* This is one of my favorite Scriptures because it's short and to the point, but there's a lot of depth in this passage. Oftentimes, the most recognizable part of the verse is to honor the Lord with the first fruits of all your produce. However, most people overlook the first part of the verse, which says, *Honor the Lord with your wealth...* Giving the Lord the first fruits of your produce is indeed a function of worship to the Lord. But let's momentarily place our focus on what it means to honor the Lord with your wealth.

If money is a tool to honor God, the million-dollar question becomes: How do we honor God financially? Consider these questions. How do you honor God with your body? How do you honor God with your marriage or within your local church? You honor Him financially in the same way: by obeying His Word and focusing on Him as we make decisions.

If we examined the most recent major purchases you've made, would we be able to conclude that you're committed to honoring God? For the moment, let's remove the major purchases and look at the smaller ones. Ask yourself the same question: Are those purchases focused on God? In general terms, does pornography honor God? Does the casino honor God? How about drugs? How about profane and sexually explicit movies and music? What about investing money in companies that have questionable business practices? One of the easiest ways to honor God financially is to do our best to only spend money in places and on things that can actually give God honor and glory. As my pastor often says, "The best funded army always wins the war."

At the end of every purchase, consider who got a tick mark in the win column. We can speak until we're blue in the face about how much we support or desire certain things. Ultimately, how we spend our dollars directly speaks to what we truly support and value. Outside of daily living, we are often presented with the opportunity to help with missions, help out a family or relative in need and give to our local church. These are the very things that not only bring God much glory, but also display our care for others based on how we spend our money.

What is Wealth and How Do We Build It?

Throughout this book, you will see me reference the importance of working with professionals for individualized advice, but I think it's also important to have some general guidelines to help you evaluate how to build wealth from a holistic view. There are 6 areas of wealth management, all of which we will deal with in the book. To build wealth, you must be aware of how these 6 areas impact each other. Each is built on one another, but it's vital for the financial stability of your family, community, and the kingdom that there be a solid foundation.

1. Risk Management: Risk management deals with the major financial risks associated with living, or the what-ifs that can derail any financial plan. These risks are often associated around 3 areas that can be solved partly or completely through proper levels of insurance:

a. Disability Insurance– Insurance designed to replace lost income associated with an interruption in work due to injury or illness. Think of this as paycheck insurance.

b. Life Insurance – Insurance designed to address the risk associated with the loss of income due to death (there are other planning aspects discussed.

c. Long-Term Care Insurance – Insurance designed to provide income to pay for medical expenses such as nursing homes or in- home care that results from a long-term illness. LTC insurance is designed to help protect against the depletion of assets due to medical costs that often come with old age and/or sickness/illness.

Risk management is the foundation of wealth management. No matter how great of a saver someone may be or how savvy an investor they are, if these risks are not planned for and the undesirable happens, it may be very difficult to build wealth beyond those stages. Think about the widow who had to go back to work when her husband passed, or the business that closed after the owner/s died. Though tragedy can strike at any time, we often have the opportunity to plan for "what could" happen, as well as "what will" happen.

2. Financial Position: Financial position addresses things like debt, as well as emergency savings and cash flow. Essentially, financial position takes a look at where you are today. Ideally you want to have 3-6 months of monthly expenses saved to address any financial emergencies that may arise, which in a perfect scenario would keep us out of debt. Emergency funds are typically called "rainy day" funds, which comes from the analogy of if it rains, or something unpleasant or unexpected happens , you have resources set aside for it. If we were discussing a literal rainy day, this would often be shelter or an umbrella. Financially, this is often money available to pay for the busted tire, car accident, unplanned dentist trip, or leaky roof.

Once we have rainy day money, we can begin to build up our "sunny day" money. Entrepreneur, business coach, and author Myron Golden says, "a piece of paper always has two sides." Meaning, there has to be another side of the story, or contrasting view. If there is a chance something unfavorable happens, there's also a chance that something favorable happens, or nothing unfavorable happens, which is still a form of something favorable occurring. Instead of replacing a busted tire, you might want to buy a new car. Instead of needing to borrow money to cover an expense, you may want to give to help your favorite charity. Instead of worrying about how to cover an unexpected expense, you may be in a position to look at ways to grow your money through investment opportunities.

3. Investing: Once you move beyond having the proper levels of savings for an emergency fund, you can move beyond bank accounts and look at various investment opportunities.

4. Retirement Planning: Retirement Planning is all about creating income streams. Retirement will be what you make it. The quicker you can create income to support your lifestyle, that doesn't require you to go to an actual job, the quicker you can retire. This will be reviewing options like your company sponsored retirement plan, ROTH and regular IRA's, real estate, as well as the various small business retirement plans available.

5. Taxes: As you make financial decisions along the way, you must be conscious of the tax implications both now, and in the future. Tax rules have changed numerous times over the years, and being unaware can be a detriment to your long-term financial success.

6. Estate Planning: Documentation to ensure upon death or disability, the transfer of your assets is completed with as little confusion or taxes as

possible. Good estate planning should minimize your family's interactions with the public court systems or the IRS.

3   Brick I: Generating Income

I know you bought this book to learn how to biblically manage your finances and, hopefully, you haven't checked out at this point. But, in order to fully receive and apply everything you'll learn in this book, we have to uproot the deficient financial theology. Now that we've laid the foundation, we can start building the house, which is biblical wealth management. I use the word "wealth" because we often make the mistake of believing that wealth only belongs to the rich and famous. That's simply not true. We all are wealthy, but some are wealthier than others. The reason why isn't as important as the fact that we recognize we all have a measure of wealth. If we don't recognize that, we often put the burden of giving on others who we believe have more. But, let's look at how the Bible defines wealth. In Strong's Concordance, the word "wealth" has multiple meanings. However, it's all interrelated with goods, resources, substance, treasure, and strength. That's right! In some sense, our strength is directly related to our wealth. If we look at it from the sense of the church as a whole, without some sort of wealth, the church is essentially weakened. The big picture is that we all have some goods, resources and strength to utilize. We simply need to build on what we've been given.

The first step to building biblical wealth is actually generating income through *working*. I'm sure you were expecting to receive some deep secret that's only been revealed to the elite. But, this is truly the first step: *simply working*. Working can be viewed from multiple angles, but I'll start with the basic understanding of simply earning an income. You'd be surprised at how many won't embrace this concept. We believe that, because we have Christ, things should be easier. Indeed, He does make life easier, but it doesn't mean that Christ is a substitute for the things we're supposed to do. If Jesus went to the cross, surely, we should be able to go to work. Some people have no relationship with God, but simply because they work hard or run a good business, they've become wealthy.

On the flipside, we think our faith alone will propel us in all matters. I'm a person of faith. But no matter how much faith I have, if I don't generate income, I won't be able to pay my bills or put food on the table. No matter where you are financially, much of what you have, and what you will ever have, will typically come from you and your spouse's income, until you learn to invest, which we will get to later in the book. Though the Bible teaches us that we are to leave an inheritance to our children's children, many studies of millionaires and billionaires have found that much of the wealth in the world has not been inherited, which is simply unbiblical. Proverbs 13:22 says, "a good man leaves an inheritance to his children's children, while the sinner's wealth is laid up for the righteous." If no one makes the decision to create and leave wealth for future generations, each generation is left to themselves to create it, which means we have to work. We should all have a strong work ethic, but if we were to use a baseball analogy, the game can be a lot easier if we're starting from third base.

As someone who has worked more than a decade in Corporate America, I've seen how our ability to excel at work often leads to the greatest opportunities to witness for Christ. We don't have to show people or be employees of the month, but no one should be able to outwork us, because we are working for a purpose that far exceeds our paycheck. Matthew 5:16 tells us, *"In the same way, let your light shine before others, so that they may see your good works and give glory to your Father who is in heaven."*

Not only does work have a direct connection with provision, but it also has a direct connection with purpose. Though we may not recognize it, God often has us work in careers that directly tie to our greater God-given purpose. In the Bible, we see the story of Moses, who was called to lead the people of Israel to the promised land. Prior to him receiving his ministerial call from God, he was already established in his working call as a shepherd for his father-in-law's sheep. As a matter of fact, Moses was keeping the sheep when he experienced the historic event of speaking with God at the burning bush. Don't miss this. Moses received his calling and heard the voice of God *while he was at work*.

We know God is sovereign, so I don't want to pretend that He's bound by us as a people. But imagine how history could have changed if Moses wasn't on the job. What if he chose not to go to work that day? We see a very similar account with King David, who also was a keeper of sheep for his father, Jesse. The story of David is very compelling because his family, and everyone else in the town, expected one of his brothers to be anointed as Saul's successor. While his brothers and father were all cleaned up for the ceremony, David was called from the field. He was called from keeping the sheep, to receive his anointing as king. Just like Moses, David received his calling *at work*. Working is truly a blessing from God.

Throughout this book, you'll see many references to the Book of Proverbs because it's one of the wisdom books. It was primarily written by the wisest man who ever lived, King Solomon. Proverbs is more of a guide than a declaration. I don't want to give the false impression that everything you read is guaranteed to happen. However, I've yet to find someone who lives by these passages who does not fare well financially. Proverbs 14:4 says, *"Where there are no oxen, the manger is clean, but abundant crops come by the strength of the ox."* Remember, during these times, one of the main sources of wealth were crops, fields and animals. If you've ever been in a manger or on a farm, you know the general rule of thumb for maneuvering the land is, "Watch your step." If the open fields are dirty, how dirty are the stables and mangers that they live in?

Scripture shows us that it's the oxen that plow the fields and gives us the opportunity to cultivate crops, which means a consistent part of producing an abundance of crops is the undesired position of cleaning up after them. As Scripture tells us at the beginning, we have the option of having clean stables by not having any oxen. But, without the oxen, there are no crops. Without crops, the possibility of wealth could be limited. While some of us may literally have dirty, hard, undesirable jobs, this may be our primary source of building wealth right now, so let's embrace it.

Proverbs 16:3 says, *Commit **your work** to the Lord, and your plans will be established.* Notice that the passage tells us to "commit your work"—not your ideas, prayer or hopes. While there is power in prayer and hope, we're talking about taking action. Once we commit to working, the Lord will establish our plans. Our relationship with God is a two-way street. Throughout the Bible, we see many promises of God with conditions. If we do this, God will do that. Committing our work to the Lord also causes us to determine that, no matter what our job is, we'll do our part to the best of our abilities. Many people work jobs halfheartedly because they're waiting on their dream job to magically appear. But if we don't work hard now and learn, how do we ever expect to land our dream job? Everything we do is simply building blocks on top of each other. Slacking on the job does not honor God. If we're not truly giving our best effort, are we sincerely committing our work to the Lord?

I can recall working at KFC while I was in college. If I can be honest, I loathed that job. To this day, I would argue it was the worst job I ever had. I was a cook while my friends got the easy jobs of taking orders from the walk-ins and drive-through customers. My friend Dave Toney jokingly called me "birdman" and often laughed at how dirty my shoes would get. They got so dirty, my all black shell toe Adidas were called "air crispy's." When you are a cook at KFC, you are dealing with raw chicken, flour, and grease all day. When the store closed you were in charge of cleaning up the mess that was made throughout the day, which included cleaning the fryer that I burned myself on several times. I don't think I can overemphasize how much I disliked that job. I'm not trying to pick on KFC, because we all have one of those jobs that we despised. I actually appreciate my experience because it taught me to push past my feelings and give everything I do my very best, even when I don't want to be there.

Building wealth through working is going to call for sacrifice, as well as tunnel vision. You may loathe your current job to no end, but still commit your work to the Lord. Work as unto the Lord, knowing that He gave us His best in Jesus Christ. Many times, the very things we learn on our jobs are what propel us to the next season of our lives. They are often success markers, allowing us to reflect on how those situations helped us get to the place of wealth.

Throughout our lives, we should always have something that we are constantly working toward. I don't mean money. I mean purpose. Don't just get up and go to work. Your current job may be a stepping stone to the next. It's important that we don't get into a place of complacency, where we no longer sharpen our skills or strive for more. Some fields require higher education, but we must make sure we do all we can to increase our employability. Whether it's a degree, certification or program, do all you can to give yourself the greatest probability for income increases. For far too long, many of us have been just moving and doing, with no central destination in mind. Our work needs to be part of a bigger plan.

4   Brick II: Planning

As we've discovered, one of the critical points of biblical wealth building is working and generating income. Coupled closely with working is having a plan. One of the best pieces of advice I ever received can be universally applied to any situation. It's simply to start with your end goal in mind. Before you do anything, consider what the result is that you want to achieve. Prior to starting anything, think about if what you're considering will get you closer to where you want to be or pull you further away from your goal. Let's take a closer look at what planning looks like biblically.

If you were to have a discussion with ten random people, and ask them if they have goals, many of the answers should be, "Yes." But what type of answer do you think you'll get if you ask them if they have plans for those goals? No matter what we're dealing with, especially as it relates to financial matters, by far one of the main reasons why things don't get done is because we fail to plan. Amazingly, we serve an all-knowing, all-powerful God. Yet, he still had a plan, and still has a plan for His people, individually and collectively. So, if the one who knows all, the one who is everywhere and has everything has a plan, what should that suggest about those made in his image? Some people find it difficult to plan financially because it can be quite complex. I suggest starting with the very simple step of prayer. I know this probably seems too simple and possibly impractical. However, prayer is a good starting point to not only seek the Lord for *what* plans we should make, but *how* we should go about those plans.

Proverbs 16:9 says, "*The heart of man* **plans** *his way, but the Lord establishes* *his steps."* Do you see the beauty, power and relief in this Scripture? Too many of us subject ourselves to unnecessary work and worry because we try to do things on our own. Scripture teaches us to plan, and God shows us how to carry out those plans. We need to set our goals according to God's plans and He'll show us how to get things done. Our plans must be based on an end goal, just like God's plans are based on the end goal of us being redeemed to Him. Start with the end in mind. Explorer Antoine de Saint-Exupery penned one of my favorite quotes of all time:"A goal without a plan is just a wish."

Think about your financial goals. Is it to pay off debts, save for retirement or pay for your child's education? Do you need to pay for a wedding or put enough money away to retire early? Behind every goal is a financial component. Even if you set the goal of eating healthier, you're going to have to spend more money on food.

Another critical component of building biblical wealth is determining who will assist you in your journey. Just as you need to pray about setting the plan and pursuing the plan, you also need to pray about your "financial accomplices." For some, this may be a bit unnerving because this means you must be open with other people about a very intimate subject. However, for you to pursue such an important thing alone is very dangerous. Because the financial decisions we make impact more than just us, we don't need to make these decisions alone. If we do, we're essentially taking on a form of pride or arrogance. We are indirectly stating that we either don't need or desire help.

As we establish these financial plans, one of the first things we can do is seek advice from people who are financially wise. We must seek advice from those who have some experience in the areas we're trying to venture into. Too many times, people take financial advice from others who either have no experience or no financial wisdom. Yet, they have established a relationship with these people and trust them. People can mean well and still be completely wrong, so be careful who you seek counsel from. Even if you don't know everything financially about someone, we all typically have some sort of intuition about who may be doing well financially.

Wisdom is not always displayed by material things people possess. Wisdom is often found in what some people *don't have*. People who don't have debt, financial stress or friction in their marriage should be considered wise. Keep in mind that you're seeking help because you're limited. You must also know the limits of the people you're taking counsel from. Professionals, such as myself, don't know it all and we work with finances daily. As you continue to work these plans, one of the things you need to have is accountability.

While you may have multiple financial partners to help in specific areas, you want to make sure you have someone who will help keep you focused on your end goal. Sometimes, we get discouraged or off track, and that financial partner will encourage us and give us a kick in the pants, when necessary. Make sure that whomever you choose to help with your financial goals aren't biased. I'm not saying don't rely on a close friend. But you need to make sure you have someone who knows how to love you and be honest and objective at the same time.

Another critical aspect of your financial plans is to write your goal down. If it's still in your head, it's not a plan. It's called an idea. Not only does the plan need to be written out, but it also needs to have a deadline. If it stays in your head, it literally stays in your head. If there's no deadline, it becomes something that ends up floating in space until "the time is right." Chances are your life won't likely slow down at any point soon. Even if you're finishing school or another big project, something else will be jockeying for the space on the priority list. Your financial plans must have priority with a deadline.

The deadline is critical because it gives you something to aim for daily. When you wake up every day with the expectation that what you do today is going to get you closer to the plans you've made, you begin to live on purpose, with purpose. If you don't put a deadline on the plan, you'll find yourself setting the same goal over and over. The deadline is not always about the end goal, but making sure you take the actions needed to achieve the end goal.

Once you begin to plan, make sure your goals are specific. Saying, "I want to lose weight. I want to save money. I want to give to charity," are all great plans. But you need to not only know *when* you want to do these things, but *specific numbers for each category*. Otherwise, the plans will be incomplete. For instance, the necessary steps to save $10,000 will likely be different than what's needed to save $100,000 or $1,000,000. The action plan for losing 50 pounds will likely be a drastic contrast to losing ten pounds. Without knowing exactly what you want to do and when, any plans you make may be insufficient. Be specific. What I've found is when I set a specific timeframe for my plans, I've been able to accomplish them earlier than the deadline I set. When something is specific and detailed, there's an internal time-clock that's constantly ticking and reminding us we need to get to work. Allow me to show you how a plan and a *specific* plan differ.

Plan A: I want to save more money for retirement.

Plan B: I want to save $60,000 over the next six years for retirement.

Plan A: I want to get out of debt.

Plan B: I want to pay off my $10,000 of credit card debt over the next 15 months.

Plan A: I want to help my kids pay for college.

Plan B: I want to give my kids $25,000 for college by their first year of college.

As you can see, the more specific the plan is, the more likely you are to pursue it with purpose. Even if you don't achieve the goal in the time you hoped, having the specific goal still allows you to experience some achievement, which is what's most important and most impactful. In our example above, you may not save $60K over the next six years. But, you may save $50K. Instead of the six years, it may take you eight years. Instead of paying off the $10,000 in credit cards, you may pay off $8,000 over the timeframe. You may save $20,000 for your children's college tuition instead of the intended $25,000. If you don't fully reach your number, would you dare consider yourself a failure? I think not.

There's another aspect of writing down your plans that is often overlooked. Habakkuk 2:2-3 says, *And the L*ORD *answered me: "Write the vision; make it plain on tablets, so he may run who reads it. For still the vision awaits its appointed time; it hastens to the end—it will not lie. If it seems slow, wait for it; it will surely come; it will not delay.* Writing it down keeps us focused on what we're doing and why. When things go slow or get off track, even in our frustrations, our efforts won't be in vain. It's one thing to struggle, which we all are going to do at times. But it's another thing to struggle and not see any light at the end of the tunnel. Scripture teaches us that if God gives us a vision it will come at its appointed time. So, don't give up.

Lastly, when it comes to planning, you must be intentional. Nothing godly happens by accident, mistake or happenstance. We serve an intentional God. So, we must also be intentional in our attempts and pursuits. Ecclesiastes 9:10 says, *"Whatever your hand finds to do, do it with your might, for there is no work or thought or knowledge or wisdom in Sheol, to which you are going."* No matter what we do, we can't approach it haphazardly. None of us know how much time we have left on this earth. While we have the ability to plan and pursue, we need to be focused and intentional. I once heard a sound byte from Denzel Washington giving a commencement speech. In that speech, he made an analogy that stuck with me. He told a story of someone lying on their deathbed. Surrounding their bed were all their thoughts, ideas, dreams and goals that came to them during their life. The thoughts, the ideas, the dreams were mad at the person because they had to die with them. Let's not allow this to happen to us.

5   Brick III: Creating Money Systems

We've now laid the foundation, added the first brick of working and added the brick of planning on top of working. Our financial house is starting to come together. But before we get too far ahead of ourselves, we need to lay the third financial brick, which is budgeting.

Budgets often get a bad rap. However, when done correctly, budgets actually lead to financial freedom. If you're someone who cringes at the word "budget" or views them in a negative light, I want to challenge you to look at a budget in light of its capabilities, not its restrictions. The restrictions are solely in place to allow you financial freedom today and in the future. Budgets simply create a system that prioritizes and directs what happens with your money.

In all my years of financial planning, I can say the budgeting step in the planning process can often take the most time because many people don't know how much they spend on a normal basis. They know how much their mortgage or rent is, but things like gas, food, tithes and clothes are often left out or grossly underestimated.

Take yourself, for example. Write down how much you think you spend a month, even if you normally do a budget. Now write down above the number your monthly take home paycheck and subtract your expenses. Now, can you honestly say you have "that" amount of money left over each month? If that number is negative, there are other things we'll discuss that need to be addressed. The second part will take more time and you can go back to it. But I want you to go through the last three to six months of your bank statements and see how close your numbers are. You may surprise yourself. I can't tell you how many times someone has told me they take home $5,000 per month and their expenses are $3,500 per month, yet we can never seem to find that extra $1,500 per month. At times, I'm guilty of this myself. A budget is one of the most powerful tools you can equip yourself with for several reasons.

For starters, a budget is a picture of where you are today, good or bad. Regardless of where you desire to be in the future, you'll have a tough task getting there without knowing where you are today. You must know your starting point. Any steps you take should be based on either building on the good that you're already doing or taking corrective action in weak areas.

Secondarily, your budget allows you to see areas where you may be underestimating or overspending. On the surface, the two sound the same. But when I mention underestimating, take a grocery budget, for example. In our household, my wife and I budget together, but I typically pay the bills. However, one of the things my wife constantly reminds me of is the fact that I was underestimating the grocery expenses. She wasn't overspending, but the numbers that I set for our household for food just weren't reasonable for a family of 7. Overspending focuses on wasteful activities rather than necessary expenses. An example of overspending may be eating out for lunch or dinner on top of your grocery expenses. This will vary from household to household.

Thirdly, your money system allows you to know what figures you need to be accountable to. If you're going to have a financial accountability partner, you need to share and even consider creating your budget with them.

Lastly, if you're someone whose income exceeds your expenses (ideally, this is everyone), it allows you to allocate money to other areas that may be of interest like giving, retirement, education, travel, etc. Let's review some of the vital parts of creating a successful money system.

Accuracy

No matter how beautiful your numbers look on paper, if they're not accurate, it doesn't do you much good. Your numbers must be accurate. This is the very reason some people strongly dislike doing a budget because it takes time to get accurate numbers. One of the easiest things to start with for accuracy is your paystub. Whether it's electronic or you still receive a paper paystub, familiarize yourself with both your pre-tax income and your take-home pay. It's clear why you need to know your take-home pay, but knowing what you earn before taxes and other deductions is just as important. There may be some opportunities in your budget that allow you to adjust some of those pre-tax expenses, which would alter your take-home pay. For those of you who work in fields where your income fluctuates, you may have to complete a new estimate each month.

As you figure out your monthly expenses, there are various categories: household, credit cards, loans, automobile and food. You also want to consider those expenses that are fixed and fluctuate. Typically, items like your mortgage, rent and car payment are fixed payments because they typically don't change. Costs like student loans or other personal loans can also be categorized as fixed payments. Costs like utilities will fluctuate in different seasons and times. Some utility companies offer fixed payment options to keep the expenses from fluctuating too high in peak seasons. In the summer, electricity payments are going to often be higher than heating costs, but the reverse happens in the winter. If you pay both heating and electricity, these bills may simply flip-flop for you in different seasons, which may be helpful in estimating your costs.

You can also review what you spend on a particular category and take average costs throughout the year. For example, if your electricity bill is $30 for four months, $60 for four months, then $50 for another four months, you can simply take your total of $560 for the year and divide it over 12 months. Then, budget $47 per month for electricity. The same goes for those expenses you pay annually, semi-annually and quarterly, like car or homeowners' insurance. If you're paying $600 twice a year, budget $100 per month. An additional aspect of budgeting is not forgetting the things that we do on a normal basis. Because the cost may not be that large, we don't budget for it. For me, it's often my beard trim because I typically only go twice a month. It's not a large expense, but still an expense nonetheless. Car maintenance is another area where you may find it hard to budget. However, if you consider the age of your car and normal maintenance patterns, you can easily budget for car maintenance and repairs. I typically get one oil change a year, at a cost of $120 each time. That's $10.00 per month. Other maintenance costs such as tires, system flushes and brake jobs still may be applicable. So, you need to allocate extra dollars for those things on an annual basis.

Giving is another area that I often see missing from budgets. In some way, I see it as a good thing because that means people don't see it as just another bill or expense. However, it's definitely an outflow from your home, and it should be allocated as such. You'll also need to budget for personal items like deodorant, toilet paper and other household items. Lastly, take a second look at what I like to call the, "entertainment budget." This is where I find most people either don't account for at all, or they overspend. The difficult part about the entertainment budget is that you must determine what's entertainment for you. Movies, bowling, golfing and eating out with your friends and/or spouse are all key components of the entertainment expense. Another area missing on the average household budget is shopping. Of course, there may be a small budget for clothes, especially for those who wear uniforms to work. But there's also things like Christmas gifts and birthday presents for friends and relatives. These should be easier to budget for because the dates don't change. You know the date of Christmas annually and your best friend's birthday is the same every single year. Therefore, there shouldn't be any "surprise" expenses surrounding these items. Even when it comes to weddings, baby showers and family vacations, you still typically have some notice, which allows you to plan for them.

Creation

Once we know what our normal take home pay and expenses are, we can begin to create our money system. As I described earlier, you don't want to do your entire budget alone. If you're married, make sure you create your budget with your spouse, even if they don't want to do it. In most marriages, there's typically one person who may be more structured or better with money than the other, but spouses should create their system together. If you're single, it's fine to create your budget alone. However, if you feel comfortable, do it with a close friend or your accountability partner. I'm more concerned with the budget being numerically accurate than categorically accurate. If you put your movies expenses under miscellaneous instead of entertainment, it really doesn't matter as long as it's accounted for and correct. Categories of a budget may bring to your recollection items you normally didn't think about, and that's definitely a positive. But don't beat your head against a wall trying to figure out, or even create, a category. As you create your budget, you can always go the old school pen and paper route. However, I recommend using the electronic budgeting tools, especially since many of them are free.

I also like Dave Ramsey's tools for budgeting for several reasons. Dave Ramsey uses a concept called "zero-based budgeting." This concept puts a "name" on every dollar. Every dollar you have has a destination and there's really no "leftover" money. Any possible income above your expenses has a designated place. For instance, if you bring home $5,000 per month, and your expenses are $3,500, the extra $1,500 you have could be allocated as such:

- $200 given to church
- $400 paying off debt
- $300 kid's education
- $250 new car fund
- $350 towards retirement

Again, these numbers and allocations will vary based on your situation, but you can see how a zero-based budget can help you. Dave Ramsey also uses what's called the "envelope system" for certain expenses like gas and food. The idea behind the envelope system is that it's difficult to overspend with cash because you can physically hold it. Once it's gone, it's gone. If you spend $25 too much at the store, there's nothing physical to stop you with a credit or debit card. There are also different apps you can download for budgeting. If you have a computer with Microsoft Office, Excel also has various budgeting tools. Again, you'll have to determine which tools work best for you. Even if you don't have a live person to assist with your budgeting, consider these electronic tools.

What's just as important as having a budget, is having some standard benchmarks to best utilize the money you have. While everyone's situation is different, I've found some frameworks that if followed, often lead to maximizing your income no matter the dollar amount.

IRS	($0.25) $0.75
Quality of Life	($0.40) $0.35
Short Term Savings	($0.10) $0.25
Long Term Savings	($0.20) $0.05
Risk Management	($0.05) $0.00

Imagine you have $1.00 and this is how you decide to spend it. The IRS automatically takes their share of the pie, so if you're in a 25% tax bracket, we now have $0.75 cents to spend. We now allocate $0.40 cents, or 40% to our quality of life. This is going to be things like your mortgage, food, family vacations, etc. We now allocate $0.10 cents, or 10% to your short term savings. This money is primarily being put aside to make sure we have 3-6 months monthly expenses saved in the bank. We may also allocate money for other short term goals here. As we approach that 3-6 months of expenses saved, we can start to allocate these funds to long term savings. This will take time, so you can still start with your percentages above, and once you obtain the 3-6 months of expenses in savings, you can consider putting all of your savings towards long-term savings if there are no other short-term things to allocate in the plan.

We put $0.20 cents, or 20% towards long term savings such as your investments, retirement, children's education, etc. The last $0.05 cents or 5% is allocated to risk management. If you recall, these are our insurance policies that protect our income and assets from injury, illness, and death. These are life, disability, and long-term care insurance. I would encourage you to take a pause and go through this exercise based on how you're spending now. What I tend to find is that many people are high on the quality of life and low on the savings and risk management. This is not the 10 commandments, you do have some wiggle room. But if you are spending upwards of 60-70% or more on quality of life you're in the danger zone. You need to have an honest conversation with yourself and examine if you have clearly defined a need versus a want, and if you're putting enough money towards things that build wealth. Remember this doesn't happen overnight, so don't get discouraged if you don't find that you have room to save or invest. If this is your situation, your assignment is to try and increase income and lower expenses to free up money to go towards your goals. This may also call on you to change lifestyles. It could also mean you getting a different job, starting a business, increasing your education, or downsizing a house or car. I know that last part may seem uninteresting or even hard, but I assure you it's not as hard as realizing you can't retire, send your child to school, or fund the ministry that tugs at your heart. Choose your hard work wisely!!!!

Creativity

As you've figured out your monthly expenses, you can also take a step back and look for other ways to tweak your budget. You must be creative and intentional. No matter what we say, most of us have some areas where we waste money. Consider expenses that you may be able to either lower or eliminate, especially if you find yourself in the situation where your expenses exceed your income. Creativity in your budget means reevaluating what you're spending to make sure needs are actually needs and not wants.

At one point, I had multiple newspapers and magazines coming to my home. As much as I loved reading them, I didn't realistically have enough time to read them all. My wife helped me realize that I needed to cancel some of the subscriptions. In the same vein as the magazines, many people have gym memberships they don't use. This is yet another area where I was wasting money. Once my second child came along, I found it nearly impossible to get to the gym. So, I canceled the membership and bought a used treadmill and some running shoes. I saved some money and still got the job done.

My wife and I also determined that cable was no longer necessary for our family. I'm not suggesting that there's anything wrong with cable, but maybe consider switching companies to lower the expense or eliminate cable altogether. What if there's a financial goal you want to hit, and the only thing that's keeping you from hitting that goal is your cable bill? Is it worth giving up?

According to a 2015 article from Yahoo Finance, the average cable bill in the U.S. is $99 per month, or $1,200 per year. Cable over five years is now $6,000, over 10 years $12,000 and over 20 years $24,000. Over 40 years, which is the average work life for most people, you will have spent $48,000 on watching television. Though I didn't have to change my cell phone carrier, I was still able to change my plan with the company, allowing me to save $600 per year. The biggest areas where I see opportunities for many people are the daily lunches and occasional trips to the coffee house. For those who eat out and purchase coffee on a regular basis, this can total anywhere from $25 to $100 per week. Assume we're again dealing with a 40-year work life. We've eaten and drank anywhere from $52,000 to $200,000. That's a very expensive sandwich and cup of coffee. Also consider changing internet providers and shopping out your home and auto insurance. We live in a competitive business environment where companies stand ready to get your business. Switching may result in more money in your pocket. It's an investment of time that can result in thousands being returned back to your household.

Accountability

The last point I will make about your budget is going back to accountability. I'm a proponent of accountability partners. Even if you're the one holding yourself accountable, there needs to be accountability. It doesn't make sense to put yourself through the rigor of getting to this part in the budget and not following through with it. Earlier, I talked about corporations using budgets. All entities have them, but it becomes a disaster when they have them and don't stick to them. Bankruptcy for a major city like Detroit could be attributed to the city budget not being correct, followed, or a combination of both. Every dollar has an opportunity cost, and using money in one area prevents us from using the same funds in other areas. By having a budget, and strictly following it, you maximize every dollar you have. The quickest way to increase your income is to lower your expenses.

By now, you can see that biblical financial management is practical and requires work. We know the godly purpose of money and we know we must work, create plans and follow a system. As you consider the six key areas of wealth management, your ability to manage your money within a system is going to give you the greatest opportunity to utilize each area to your benefit.

6   Brick IV: Wise Counsel

As we begin to build wealth biblically, one of the things I will continue to reiterate is the need to stay focused on your goals. Do not try to achieve them alone. We've already discussed why accountability almost always improves your results and sustainability. But I want to give you a bit more support on who you should consider getting help from. As a professional, I'm sure I can't help but be somewhat biased to the profession. However, it's vital that you work with professionals. The need for a professional may come and go as you build assets and your needs change, but don't do it alone. As master marketer, Dan Kennedy, would say, "One is the worst number of them all." If you only have one thing, which, in our case, is a perspective or mentality, that "one" thing could be easily disrupted or taken away. That one perspective (your own) could also be the one thing that is standing in your way of building Biblical wealth. In my years of serving as a financial planner, I often have to work on helping my clients change their mentality around money, before we actually work on what to do with the money. The "why" must always come before the "how."

In addition to speaking with someone you trust, work with people who are well-versed in the ins and outs of financial management. While you respect your mother's opinion, your father's opinion and even that of your friends, they are likely not professionals. If you needed an operation, would you go to a doctor who does surgery on the side? Would you board an airplane with a pilot whose only experience flying is from what he/she read online? Again, my attempt is not to mitigate their value in your life, but you must know that the average person's knowledge may be limited.

I've witnessed many people suffer from bad advice from people who meant well but didn't know what they didn't know. Proverbs 11:14 says, *"Where there is no guidance, a people falls, but in an abundance of counselors there is safety."* If we had to separate this Scripture into two parts, there are two strong observations that can't be ignored. First, where there's no guidance, a people fall. We can attach this statement to anything. Throughout the Bible, we see people who tried to do things without proper biblical guidance, and they fell. Many times, I've had intentions on doing good things. However, I didn't have any sort of guidance. When it comes to money management, we need guidance. The most dangerous person, as it relates to money management, is someone such as myself. We can easily get overconfident in our ability to do things.

Through my college years and Certified Financial Planner™ education, I've had the opportunity to take multiple income tax classes. As a result, I could prepare my own taxes. Some years, I did my taxes myself, but I still missed some deductions. I simply either didn't know, or I didn't keep up with changes in the tax codes. I worked with an accountant for years, but thought, "I got this." In turn, it cost me money. Don't be cheap! The few dollars you may save from not working with a professional will likely not come close to the amount of money you may lose from drastic mistakes or not having professional guidance. You risk missing out on opportunities you may have not known were financially available. There's a saying that says, "Some people have financial advisors because they have money, and some people have money because they have financial advisors."

Before I get too far off from our Scripture, let's look at the second part of the verse that says, *"...but in an abundance of counselors there is safety."* Notice it doesn't say a *counselor*, but in an abundance of *counselors*, there is safety. There will likely be times in your life when you will have to make financial decisions with advice from different people. We'll touch on this more in the retirement planning section of the book, but there are typically three people you want to have at your disposal, even if you don't use them all the time. It's who I like to call the "personal dream team." You need an accountant, a lawyer and a financial advisor. Believe it or not, this could be the same person. My personal preference is to work with someone who is not wearing too many hats and spreading themselves thin. It doesn't mean this type of person can't fulfill your needs; it's my personal preference to work with specialists as opposed to generalists. Many of the decisions you make in one area affect other areas, especially for small business owners. There may be times in your future where all these people are present in the same meetings. This is what I like to call the "dream scenario," as this is how many wealthy families operate.

The final observation that I will mention from this verse is when it says that safety comes from these counselors. According to the Strong's Concordance, the Hebrew word for safety is yesha (Yeh-shaw), which means security, salvation, or welfare. These words should excite you because there's two parts to this safety and welfare. There's the idea of what safety keeps us *from*, but also what safety takes us *to*. Working with a professional could not only keep you from making big mistakes, but also give you peace from knowing you're following Scripture to pursue your goals the way God instructs us.

Another Scripture that goes hand in hand with this one is Proverbs 15:22, which states, *"Without counsel plans fail, but with many advisers they succeed."* Essentially, the two Scriptures are very close in meaning, but not exactly. They both suggest where we'll be without guidance. But, whereas one talks about safety with advisors, this Scripture speaks on success, which is what we're all after. I don't mean success in the sense of the world's definition, which may include a six-figure job, a fancy car, two and a half kids with a dog and white picket fence in your dream home. Biblical success is all tied to our obedience to God's Word, despite the end results.

Building your dream team is just the beginning. You still must put the advice and plan to work. There's nothing more frustrating than having someone seek you for advice, only for that person not to follow the advice. This isn't privy to just finances. I'm sure you can think of a situation where you've given someone advice they need, only to see them not take it and pay the price for it. As you build your plans, make sure you take the next step and put the plans to work. As we've heard, you plan your work and work your plans.

Proverbs 21:5 says, *"The plans of the <u>diligent</u> lead surely to abundance, but everyone who is hasty comes only to poverty."* The Hebrew word for diligence speaks of someone who is incisive, determined and eager. As one of my favorite preachers, the late and great J. Vernon McGhee, would say, "The Holy Spirit can't work with lazy." The Scripture also speaks on those who are hasty or impulsive. Many people are quick to pursue the fast money or quick gain, and in the end, these things lead to poverty. Things like going to the casino or playing the lottery would fall into this category. I'm not trying to shame you if that's what you do, especially for those who do it casually. But, for some people, this is a habit weekly, if not daily. Playing the lottery and other forms of gambling are essentially get-rich-quick schemes. As we see throughout the Bible, get-rich-quick schemes only lead to poverty. It's through wisdom and diligence that wealth is accumulated, not by chance or fate. Remember, it's not the plans of the lazy, the timid, the undisciplined, or even the schemer that leads to abundance. It's the plans of the diligent.

7 Brick V: Saving

Saving directly impacts all six areas of wealth management, but you can see this directly with financial positioning, as well as investments and retirement planning. The interesting thing is that when many people speak of wealth, they often refer to it as building wealth because there must be a foundation established. Wealth doesn't come out of thin air, nor by guessing and wishing. It's strategic.

We now know God's purpose for money. We've also established the fact that we as Christians need to work diligently. We also learned how to honor God financially. We've also covered how important it is to focus on financial planning and budgeting. Now we can move on to one of the foundations of building wealth: saving.

At this point, you're likely already beginning to save, even if it's not as much as you would like to save. Earlier in the book, we talked about the difference between wants and needs. If we don't truly get a grip on needs versus wants, we'll struggle in areas we don't need to. Whether it's coming from well-respected people like Warren Buffett, or me, the key to saving is living below your means. Whatever we do financially says more about our hearts and minds than anything else. Many of the things we do financially (especially if they're bad habits) are often a result of emotional, physical, and/or spiritual instability. I can attest to this personally.

Growing up in a household where many of the things I wanted weren't available because our family didn't have the money, ultimately resulted in bad habits as a young adult. I had a few dollars and available credit. So, whenever there was something that I wanted to get, I went and got it. The same reason that someone would eat a tub of ice cream by themselves is often the same reason why some of us make poor financial decisions. A large reason why some can't successfully build wealth is because they feel they must look a certain way or have certain possessions. The world tells you that you've arrived once you receive certain titles, stature, income levels and degrees. But, let's look at what the Word says. Proverbs 12:9 says, *"Better to be lowly and have a servant than to play the great man and lack bread."* As you can see, many times when we make decisions financially, it is often rooted in wanting to feel a certain way or look the part compared to other people. We seek to fit into certain crowds that we find socially acceptable. We need to have a sense of humility as we build wealth. Humility can be expressed financially. As the Word tells us, many of us are lacking bread because we're too focused on being highly thought of by others. I would caution you again on trying to keep up with The Joneses because they could very well be broke or actually wearing their wealth. Most real wealth can't be adorned on you.

    As someone who works with affluent clients, let me give you some insight into how many of them think and approach life in general. For one, many don't wear their wealth. The majority of people who I've met or done business with that would be considered wealthy or affluent don't often look like it. Of course, some of them may drive expensive cars, and that's their choice. Though they may have some of these "signs of wealth," they view material things from an opportunity and investment cost standpoint.

    When they approach spending money, they often consider what they *won't* be able to do should they spend even a small amount of money on certain items. If they spend $100,000 on a Benz, what would that prevent them from doing? Or does it make more sense to buy a $25,000 or $50,000 car and use the other $50,000 or $75,000 to do something else more profitable? I use the word "profitable" because, with the exception of rare and classic cars, cars almost always lose their value the moment you drive them off the lot. So, from an investment standpoint, does it make sense to spend more on a car that you know will lose value, or put it into a vacation home, investment, or business expenditure that has a much greater chance to increase in value, which grows your wealth? Their clothes are typically no different than the average person's. Unless someone works in a profession that requires fancy clothes, their clothes are plain.

Another aspect that the wealthy bring to the table is, when making financial decisions, they're typically looking at the big picture. Many of my clients have foregone the opportunity to enjoy certain pleasures of more expensive items because they knew spending too much money on material goods was not wise. Instead, they used that money to help their children or different foundations.

I can recall someone telling me, "Maurice, do you know when you have enough money?" I, of course, obliged his request, though I had a clue of where he was going. His reply may be surprising to you. He said, "When you can afford anything you want, and still not buy it." When you can afford your wants, but continue to make decisions based on your needs, that's powerful. This may not be new to you. But some of us know better and yet continue down this road of destruction. Proverbs 15:32 states, *Whoever ignores instruction despises himself, but he who listens to reproof gains intelligence.* Sometimes we know we shouldn't make certain decisions, but it feels good so we keep going. We know we can't afford that house or that car. We know we shouldn't do the things we do with our money, yet we do it anyway. We're doing nothing but despising ourselves. Better yet, we're hurting ourselves, our families, our communities, and our church.

I'll give you the benefit of the doubt. You may not know better, so today may be your first day of instruction. Make sure you heed correction and gain understanding. I love sitting and talking with our seniors in society because they were born in a different era, so they approach money differently. For the average person in their 70s or above, they didn't have access to credit like we do today. Many of them weren't born into households where both parents worked. Because of that, many of them raised their families the same way. They couldn't do what we do today because they knew if they got behind on the bills, or overspent, or didn't save for retirement, there was no back up. They couldn't do anything else but wait on the next payday, which was often two weeks later. Credit wasn't readily available for things other than homes and cars. There was a direct need and requirement to save if you wanted something. As we mentioned earlier, the easiest way to give yourself a raise is to lower your expenses. Imagine having a constant surplus financially. It gives fuel to financial plans and only accelerates your path to financial freedom. But, to see your plans come to life, you must save your money with the intent of investing, which we will talk about later. Remember, you have the foundation of purpose, working, planning, budgeting and working with a professional. But you must save to do all these things.

Savings is one of the primary things we need to do as it relates to life financially. If you want to start a business, you must save or invest money to start the business and keep it running. If you want to pay for your child's education, you must save for it. If you want to have a more enjoyable retirement, you must save and invest for your retirement. As you will see, one of the primary reasons God tells us to save our money is to prepare for different seasons of life. It may not be starting a business or paying for a child's education, but it could be a layoff down the road that we don't see yet. We see in the Bible that saving is what preserved Egypt through Joseph's ability to interpret Pharaoh's dream. Genesis 41:29-36 recounts this event.

"There will come seven years of great plenty throughout all the land of Egypt, but after them there will arise seven years of famine, and all the plenty will be forgotten in

the land of Egypt. The famine will consume the land, and the plenty will be unknown in the land by reason of the famine that will follow, for it will be very severe. And the doubling of Pharaoh's dream means that the thing is fixed by God, and God will shortly bring it about. Now therefore let Pharaoh select a discerning and wise man and set him over the land of Egypt. Let Pharaoh proceed to appoint overseers over the land and take one-fifth of the produce of the land of Egypt during the seven plentiful years. And let them gather all the food of these good years that are coming and store up grain under the authority of Pharaoh for food in the cities and let them keep it. That food shall be a reserve for the land against the seven years of famine that are to occur in the land of Egypt, so that the land may not perish through the famine."

We can see firsthand the blessings that came from saving. Pharaoh not only placed Joseph over Egypt, but we also see Joseph being reconciled to his brothers and father. We know one of the main themes of Joseph's life is how God can turn around bad situations for our good and His glory. But don't miss what brought his brothers and father to Egypt. There was a famine in the land and they had to travel to Egypt because they knew Egypt saved their resources for this very reason and season. When we save wisely, we're a blessing to others, as well as ourselves. So, don't be surprised if God uses you the same way he used Joseph to rescue Egypt.

We can also take a note from nature on how saving works. Look at the squirrels. Like many animals, we may see very little squirrels in the winter. Yet, we see them in the fall, storing up their nuts and stashing them away for the season. They know if they're going to survive the winter, they must store up. Once winter comes, it's too late to save. The same is true for any financial goal we have. If we wait until the moment that we need the money, it's too late. You may argue that squirrels know their seasons because it's the same every year, while life for us can be unpredictable. I can agree with you on some level. We also have things that we know are coming up, yet we don't always properly save for them. Birthdays and Christmas come every year, however, we often forget to set money aside for these occasions. At some point, we want to retire or leave money to our children. Yes, some things come up unexpectedly, but those are generally the exception rather than the rule.

Take ants, for another example. Ants are typically known for two things: strength and work. As a matter of fact, the Bible even admonishes us to learn lessons from the ant. Proverbs 6:6-8 says, *Go to the ant, O sluggard; consider her ways, and be wise. Without having any chief, officer, or ruler, she prepares her bread in summer and gathers her food in harvest.* There's a lot that can be pulled from this, but notice that the Word calls the ant wise. The ant knows it must store up for the season(s) when it can't gather. It also knows it can't consume another season's resources today. For us, the seasons we must prepare for may be retirement, a child's college education, a job layoff or an illness. As children of God, we have the ability to directly receive God's will through prayer and the Bible, but the ant is considered wise because ants don't have those luxuries. Yet, they know what to do in various seasons of life. The Scripture also shows us that the ant is still working in different seasons. The ant does not take days off. It prepares in one season and gathers in another. If squirrels and ants know what to do to survive, surely, we can take steps to not only survive, but actually thrive.

Saving takes a lot of consistency. But we can't afford *not* to save. As I mentioned before, one of the foundations of being able to save is having a proper system for our money. Hopefully by now, it's become clearer (if it wasn't previously) why I placed budgeting before savings. The budget is what keeps us on track and gives us the ability to intentionally save. Many of the Scriptures presented here are out of the Book of Proverbs. Proverbs 24:27 says, *"Prepare your work outside; get everything ready for yourself in the field, and after that build your house."* Prepare your work (planning, budgeting, visions), get everything ready, then build your house. It's all about the process.

Like your 401(K) or other retirement plan contributions, consider having payroll deductions deposited into your savings account. This money would still come out of your check after tax, but most places will allow you to split your deposits to various accounts. Designate a set amount (that was previously budgeted) and have it sent to a savings account each time you receive a paycheck. Note: Pay attention to whether funds will be deposited on a dollar basis or a percentage basis.

For instance, if your payroll department allows you to set a dollar amount (i.e., $50) per pay, if your net pay is usually $2,000, after savings, your net pay will be $1,950. If you've already budgeted this amount for savings, it's not going to make any difference in funds you're using from month to month. It simply takes the extra step of you physically putting the money into savings out of the equation. If your job requires you to put a percentage of your pay into savings accounts, triple check your calculations. You don't want to make the mistake of thinking what should be a dollar amount was a percentage, and you end up moving $1,000 into savings every time you get paid instead of $50. To determine the accurate percentage, you want to put into savings, take the dollar amount you want to save per check and divide it by your net pay.

In our example, we would take $50 and divide by $2,000, giving us 2.5%. As you fill out your percentage for savings, you would simply select 97.5% of your check to go to checking and 2.5% to go to savings. If the savings account only allows whole numbers, round up, not down. If you can afford it, it's better to save $60 (3%) per check instead of $40 (2%) per check and underfund your goals.

If you're not comfortable doing this with your employer, you can do this at your local bank. Though the bank will likely not be able to do a payroll deduction, you can still set up automatic deposits to your savings account as often as you want. You just want to remember these funds are coming from your checking account. Set the deposit date a few days after your paycheck is deposited. For instance, if you receive income on the 1st and the 15th of the month, schedule your deposit into your savings account on the 5th and the 20th. As you consider saving, you can always do it manually as you receive your paychecks. However, it's wise to automate this as much as you can.

Another option to keep you on track is to make your money hard to get to. One of the reasons many people aren't saving is because they don't have a savings account. They keep all their money in a checking account and typically find that money "disappears" because it's not separated for a specific purpose. One of the first things you can do to make your savings more difficult to access is opening a savings account at a separate bank from where you do your primary banking. If you use online banking, make sure it's from a reputable bank that you trust. When the money is online, it often becomes out of sight and out of mind. Using an online account for savings may also keep you from touching the funds simply because it may take a few days to receive the money. This may keep you from making last-minute withdrawals. If you're not comfortable with an online bank, and you prefer a brick-and-mortar bank, do not only consider using a bank where you don't already bank. Consider using a smaller bank or even a credit union. A smaller bank and/or credit union may not have as many branches as larger banks, which would make it inconvenient and possibly an outright hassle for you to get the money.

I knew of someone who opened a savings account in college, which was in a neighboring state. Even after graduation, they never closed the account, allowing them to fight the temptation to use the money. In this circumstance, they would have had to travel three hours to access those funds. Needless to say, not only did that money stay there, but they continued to put money in the account on a regular basis. You may think this is a little extreme, and you're right. But if you're serious about achieving your financial goals, you must take extreme measures at times.

8 Brick VI: Giving

I know this may seem odd to you that giving is considered an intricate part of biblical wealth management; but let me expound on how and why it's in the right place. Central to wealth building is giving. Giving to God and giving to others on behalf of God is critical. This may be the most challenging topic of everything you read in this book. The subject of money is very private, sacred and outright uncomfortable for some. However, giving comes in many forms. Let's examine a few reasons we give.

- **God Has Empowered Us to Give.**

    Proverbs 3:27 says, *Do not withhold good from those to whom it is due, when it is in your power to do it.* One of the key things I've learned is that every dollar that comes into our hands is not meant to stay there. We constantly should ask God as we receive financial blessings, "What is this for?" Many times, God gives us money to give to others—be it family, friends, church or the community. As a result, these same persons may suffer if we're disobedient. Much of the time we receive money, especially if it's unexpected, we never approach it with someone else in mind. As we seek God for financial blessings and wisdom, how many times do we pray for those blessings just to have the ability to give? As God grants those requests, we, by default, end up withholding good from those who we are supposed to sow into.

- **It's God's Universal System.**

    Proverbs 11:25 (NIV) says, *A generous person will prosper; whoever refreshes others will be refreshed.* Let's be clear. We don't give because we're looking for a return, but to be gracious and obedient to God. Whenever we give, we will see a biblical form of reciprocity. In every season of my life where God has called my family to give beyond our norm, He's always surpassed what we gave in multiple forms. Remember, we're giving back to God. For Christians, Scripture teaches us that the earth is the Lord's and the fullness thereof (Psalm 24:1). If this is true, all we're doing is giving back to Him what already belongs to Him. As we give, it's critical to remember that we give to God first, then to people—naturally, as well as spiritually. We give to people because, even though the money we give touches the hands and lives of others, we're doing it to honor God first and to bless people secondarily.

    Often, we let our humanity get in the way of giving. We live in a fallen world and we all have areas where we fall short of God's standard. Oftentimes, because we may know, suspect and see the faults of others, it prevents us from giving to them. This is typically the main reason why people who regularly attend church don't give to the church. These are legitimate concerns because, far too often, churches haven't been financially transparent, or they've shown poor stewardship. Others simply don't give because they know the pastor is imperfect. All of us have our issues and often, within the church, we see leaders' flaws easier than we see our own. Again, I'm not telling you to ignore the obvious, but our humanity shouldn't interfere with us giving. That's not how God gives to us. Even in our sin and downfalls, God continues to provide our needs and often exceeds them. Giving is not about money; it's about the heart. If we don't have a problem paying GMAC or Ford Credit for a car, Capital One or Macy's for credit cards, or utility bills, but we have a problem with giving to godly causes, we must search our hearts to find out why. You must wholeheartedly examine whether or not you are attending the right church or giving to the right causes. If we have an issue with a particular church or cause that we think is purposefully mishandling money, we must ask ourselves why we're still there. We must pray that God gives us guidance on where we may need to move and when. Remember, we give unto God and God gives to us. Many times, God gives to us by the hands of others, whether that be in money or other natural means. This is not an attempt to guilt or condemn you, but to help you understand why giving is necessary. It is a beautiful, godly thing.

- **God Honors Generosity.**

As Christians, everything we do needs to be led by the Holy Spirit. However, we must be even more led by God as we give because there are times where giving could get in the way of what God wants to do. We could be giving to people who either don't genuinely need our help, or people who don't need our help in the form in which we are trying to provide. Think about all the causes we give to on a normal basis. Whether it's cancer research, childhood diabetes or even poverty, how can we give billions of dollars to these causes, yet see very little progress in the form of improvement? As a matter of fact, it seems that many of these conditions are getting *worse*.

Most of us have an innate desire to give. I'm sure that if you have a room of 100 people and asked them to recall any situation where they wanted to give financially, and they couldn't, I'm confident 75-80 people in the room would raise their hand. God has wired us to be givers. However, we must be careful that giving doesn't become superior to the Word of God, which is the main thing we need to give to others. We see an example of this very conundrum in Mark's account of Mary Magdalene pouring the expensive perfume on Jesus' feet. The disciples rebuked her and scolded her, telling her that she could have sold the perfume and given the money to the poor. But many misunderstand Jesus' response: *"You'll always have the poor with you."* Proverbs 19:17 says, *Whoever is generous to the poor lends to the Lord, and he will repay him for his deed.* But Jesus said that Mary did what was right, according to their situation.

Throughout the Bible, God has always admonished His people to care for those who are in weak or vulnerable positions. However, that isn't a substitute for the gospel. If we give financially, we should also offer the Gospel of Jesus Christ. One time, someone close to me asked me to borrow a particular amount of money. Not only was I willing to honor their request, but I was willing to give it to them because I knew the scenario they were in. I understood that they really didn't have the funds to repay me. As I prayed about the situation, I could overwhelmingly feel the presence of the Lord telling me not to do it. I don't really know why, but I can only speculate that I truly believe God wanted to show this person something that would've been lost had I given them the money. In no way am I comparing myself to the situation with Jesus, the disciples and Mary Magdalene, but I think the themes are the same. We need to make sure we seek God's will and purpose in any situation before we give.

- **It's Not Ours to Keep.**

Sometimes, I think we forget the very source of our wealth. As we already learned in Deuteronomy, it is God who gives us the ability to attain wealth. But as we grow in wealth, we sometimes believe that it's ours. Not only do we start to believe we're the source of the wealth, but we start to believe that it's ours and therefore, we can do whatever we want with it. Psalm 24:1 says, *The earth is the LORD's and the fullness thereof, the world and those who dwell therein.*

Psalms reminds us that God has created all things for His purpose. Whether it's our family, our friends, the field by our house or our money, it all belongs to Him. If it's His, we must make sure that we manage it the way He desires us to. That's why you'll see me say throughout this book that money really isn't about money. It's a matter of what we truly value and what we believe to be the most valuable. On most levels, giving is a matter of our trust. It's an area that God has continued to challenge me. I must trust Him enough to give the way He instructs me to give.

- **We've Been Recipients of Giving.**

    Throughout the Bible, one of the underlying and apparent themes is God is a giver. He's a giver of grace (giving us what we don't deserve) and mercy (not giving us what we do deserve). One of the hallmark Scriptures shows God giving. John 3:16 states, *For God so loved the world, that he **gave** his only Son, that whoever believes in him should not perish but have eternal life.* Notice that God gave Jesus to us—not that we deserved it—but He chose to give. We also see Jesus reminding us that no one can take His life, but that He chose to lay it down. He chose to give His life for us. Genesis tells us that we are made in God's image. That means we all have been wired to give. When we don't give, or have problems with giving, we aren't fully bearing the image of God. The very heart of God is to give. We see this as Jesus sends out His disciples on their first mission in the tenth chapter of Matthew. Jesus charges them to, *"Heal the sick, raise the dead, cleanse those who have leprosy, drive out demons. Freely you have received; freely give."* Do you feel that God has freely given to you? This isn't just a story; Jesus is directly speaking to His disciples. He reminds them that He chose them, He has given to them, and they need to do the same to others.

    Our giving touches lives. Just as the disciples, we've freely been recipients of grace and we need to give the same. I understand that giving is challenging sometimes because it deals with our humanity. But, in the process, we sometimes forget about the big picture. Not just from the standpoint of heavenly purposes, but when we don't give, our local church and community suffers. I've been told on more than one occasion that 20% of a normal congregation carries the financial weight of the church, which is far from God's intention. When we look at the first churches, we see the exact opposite. We see those who are so grateful for the original apostles and the early church that they are eager to give to their local church.

In Acts 4:32-35, we see, *Now the full number of those who believed were of one heart and soul, and no one said that any of the things that belonged to him was his own, but they had everything in common. And with great power the apostles were giving their testimony to the resurrection of the Lord Jesus, and great grace was upon them all. There was not a needy person among them, for as many as were owners of lands or houses sold them and brought the proceeds of what was sold and laid it at the apostles' feet, and it was distributed to each as any had need.* We don't see this every day, nor do I believe God calls us to give like this all the time. However, this passage says those who believed (i.e. Christians) were of one heart and soul, and no one said that any of the things that belonged to him was his own, but had everything in common.

Essentially, everyone viewed and approached money and possessions the same way: biblically. This was a spiritual thing. This was also in response to the apostle's testimony. It seems they were giving out of gratitude for receiving the Gospel. Thirdly, it shows these early followers of Christ pulled their resources together and no one was in need. This is the ultimate goal of giving: that people wouldn't be in need, not to affirm and give to people's wants. It's an amazing feat to consider that people sold houses and land to generate income to support the church and its members. The challenge to give never stops. It just changes over time.

- **Resistance to Giving.**

    The apostles were the leaders of the early church. Those who sold the land and homes felt secure enough to entrust them with these possessions. Maybe these same early followers saw these leaders handle other situations with sacrifice and integrity, or maybe they saw them lead the way. We see Barnabas, who was one of the early leaders in the church, mentioned in Acts as being amongst those who took part in this special giving. Maybe as Luke penned this story, he wanted folks to know that this special giving was not just the flock, but also the leaders. This story is a major challenge for all church leaders. Would your congregation feel comfortable doing the same if God called for this same type of sacrifice in your church, or is the leadership within your church the reason people don't want to give? Are we modeling financial modesty and good financial stewardship? Are we personally showing the same sacrifice and generosity that we ask and expect of our members, or are we being financial hypocrites? We must own up to our end and search our hearts for the reasons why we don't give. Sometimes, it's just our attachment to our needs, wants and possessions that stands in the way. Throughout the Bible, we're warned not to seek to get rich, not to put our trust in money, and not to become too attached to possessions. Several passages support this, and they both involve a rich person: one being old and one being young.

    In Matthew 19, we see the young ruler who approached Jesus to ask Him, *"Teacher, what good deed must I do to have eternal life?"* Jesus essentially told the young man to follow the Law of Moses. The young man told Jesus that he'd done that since he was a youth, but that's where we know the story turns. Jesus then told him to sell his possessions, give to the poor, and follow Him. God cares for the poor; otherwise, Jesus never would have told him to give his possessions to the poor. For some of us, we are the rich young ruler, though we may not be rich monetarily. Some of us may have very little possessions, yet we have a deep attachment to them. This may be why so many of us won't give or some of us believe we don't have anything to give.

In Luke's Gospel (ch.16), we see the parable of the rich manager, who hoarded all his possessions. As he got more, he built bigger barns to store all his goods. But then, he died. Jesus called him the foolish manager. He was foolish because he put his hope, comfort and personal gratifications in his possessions. But, the very thing he should've been concerned about (his soul), he neglected. Money can only do so much. Please don't get lost in the narrative of these two gentlemen being rich. Many people are wealthy and are very generous, just as there are those who have little in the form of possessions and are still very generous. On the other hand, there are those who are like the foolish manager. There are those who hoard, only to die— never having done anything profitable with what they had. Anything can turn into an idol, and money can sneakily become an idol. Determining whether or not money is an idol is not based on how much you have, but your mentality around it.

What you may have noticed that's missing from this portion of the book is an exhaustive discussion on tithing. It's not that I don't think we should tithe, or that I don't think it's important. What I don't want to do is put burdensome restrictions on what God leads you to do. The bottom line is that we should all give. How much and when we give is something that must be led by the Lord. If we view tithing in proper biblical context, we know that the 10% was a mandate put on the nation of Israel concerning much of their possessions. God required the first fruits to be given back to Him for the purpose of serving His people. While there is no Scripture in the New Testament requiring a tithe, we do see the Apostle Paul telling the church in Corinth to "set something aside" at the beginning of each week for the very purpose of carrying out the duties of ministry. We also see the Apostle Paul remind the believers of his church in Corinth of the Scripture from Deuteronomy that says a worker is worthy of his wages. The pastor or leader of the church has a right to not only be supported by his local congregation, but it is the church's responsibility to care for them.

Let's look back to Genesis when Joseph was made the overseer of Egypt's crops. Joseph didn't store away a tenth. He put away 1/5, or 20% of what he took in. As believers of the new covenant, I would dare say that we are not under any mandates of a specific percentage of our income. If you're looking for guidance on what you should give, first pray and see what the Lord would have you to do. The 10% may be a good starting point, but we shouldn't be dogmatic about it for three reasons.

For one, by stating a hard percentage every time, we completely remove the leading and power of the Holy Spirit to lead us to sow greater seeds. If you're willing to follow Christ, He will call you to give on special occasions throughout your life, which will often be in addition to your normal giving. We shouldn't make people who don't have 10% to give feel guilty, to the point where they likely won't give at all. They feel like God won't honor what they do.

While some people can't give because of their history of poor decisions, and there are others who genuinely don't have it to give. You should still feel free and good about your giving, regardless of the amount. There is freedom in giving. What you give will be up to you and God. The best example for how we, as new covenant Christians, should give is in 2 Corinthians 9. There's a familiar passage that we've heard a million times: God loves a cheerful giver. What's often ignored is the beginning of the verse where Paul wrote that, "One must give as he decided in his own heart." The following verse does indeed say whoever sows sparingly will also reap sparingly, and whoever sows bountifully will also reap bountifully. But, as we've discussed up to this point, what you give is a matter of the heart. Be genuine in your giving, and God will honor it. As we grow in our understanding and application of his word to our money, he will give us greater opportunities to give.

Lastly, I will borrow a story from the late, great Dr. J. Vernon McGhee from Thru the Bible. One of his friends frankly told him that if he only gave 10%, he would be robbing God. What a declaration that God has blessed this man so much that he feels 10% is not enough! You can give 10% of every flow of income and still have a contentious heart towards giving. You can also give 10% and be in complete disobedience to God if he's calling you to do more. I know that's the case for many of us. Giving is a spiritual gift. So, many of us are going to be challenged to give much more than 10% because it's embedded in who God made us to be. Pray, be led by the Spirit and give with the right heart.

9 Spiritual Reasons to Invest

Let's recap on what we've learned up to this point. I do this, not to be redundant, but to encourage you that this is a step-by-step process. No matter where you are in the process, if you still have breath in your lungs, you have the opportunity to change course and your desired outcome. Wealth is not an overnight get-rich-quick scheme. It's a series of calculated decisions that affect each other. This process may require you to go back and fix a couple of steps, which is perfectly fine.

The foundation is, of course, knowing the purpose of money and honoring God financially. Once we've determined that we'll honor God financially, we can transition into the practical side through working, creating systems, and planning. Once we've begun to work, budget and plan, we'll naturally see some fruit from our labor, which gives us the ability to make the transition into building wealth biblically. Note: There are many ways to achieve wealth, but not all of them are biblical.

Plans are not guarantees but making plans will give you a much higher chance of success. Remember to stay the course. Staying the course does not mean being an ostrich and burying our heads in the sand. We don't have to become the type of people who are overly optimistic and completely naïve to what's going on around them. On the contrary, your plans may have to change altogether. The course of action that you take to go after your goals may change over time. The Bible doesn't teach us to be naïve. It teaches us again and again about the importance of diligence, above most things. Proverbs 12:11 says,

"Those who work their land will have abundant food, but those who chase fantasies have no sense." Again, this teaches the heart of what the Bible shows us concerning wealth. We must work for it. Notice the Word says that those who **work** their land will have abundant food. Today, this may not mean actual land. It could be those who work their jobs or work to build their businesses.

The second part of this verse once again dispels the "name it and claim it" themes sweeping the world. While we often covet what others have, many times, it's just the mere fact that these people have worked their land. This is one of my pet peeves with the media because the media encourages you to despise those who've done well financially. The media plants seeds that suggest that everyone in those positions has done wrong or used shady practices to get where they are. In other words, you're sold on the idea that everything for you is just a fantasy and you have no way of making it yourself. For this very reason, some of us get caught up in get-rich-quick schemes and get burned trying to do something overnight.

Scripture teaches us that when we chase fantasies like the casino, lottery and Ponzi schemes, we lack sense. Another one of my favorite Scriptures in the same vein is Proverbs 14:23, which says, *"All hard work brings a profit, but mere talk leads only to poverty."* Notice it says, "all hard work." So, don't be dismayed if you're not in your current dream job that you believe makes a lot of money. You're not alone. Only a small percentage of wealth is inherited. Most of it must be created. I know people who have never made over $50,000 in one year; yet, they still became millionaires, simply by living by the principles outlined in this book. No matter what you do and where you are in life, make the most of it.

You can honor God in almost all lines of work. Work hard because it will bring a profit. Profit doesn't have to scream millions, either. But if you work hard, you should see some type of increase in your life. If you go to the gym five days a week, you should, at some point, see bigger muscles or a smaller waistline. If you practice the piano ten hours a week for a year, you should become a better piano player. The same goes for your finances. If you've grasped the concept and purpose of money, honored God financially with first fruits, worked, planned, budgeted, saved and given, you should see some type of profit. Remember: This profit is only available to those who put in the work. As we continue our journey on biblical wealth building, it's important to know why one needs to invest both spiritually and naturally, as well as your investment options.

Four Spiritual Reasons to Invest

As I've mentioned throughout this book, everything that I tell you will be supported with Scripture, which means there's both a spiritual side and natural application to what we learn throughout scripture. Your money is no different. For this very reason, I think it's worth taking a pause and noting four primary reasons that not only support why we should invest our money, but I believe the following Scriptures will support a mandate on our end. As you approach investing, there are a couple of things I want you to keep in mind.

No matter how complicated some people try to make it, financial management doesn't have to be complex. Work with professional financial advisors. Proverbs 15:22 tells us that plans fail because of a lack of counsel, Ecclesiastes 4:9-12 tells us that two are better than one. You shouldn't do this alone. Within the retirement planning process, I'll talk more in depth about the steps to finding a financial advisor and building an investment plan. But before you hire an advisor, you should have a basic understanding of what some of your investment options are. We'll touch on those after we review why we should invest, from a spiritual and natural aspect: These are the four primary spiritual reasons we should invest:

- Slow or Unexpected Seasons
- Advancing the Kingdom
- Leaving an Inheritance
- It's God's Expectation of Us

Slow or Unexpected Seasons

Some of this may seem a bit redundant, but I assure you there's multiple reasons for reintroducing topics. Some of the same reasons why we save are the same reasons why we should invest. Recall Proverbs 6:6-8 and the story of the ant. The ant intuitively knew that seasons in its life constantly changed. You must set provision aside for those very reasons. While I understand that legitimate things happen that we don't expect, there are other times where we should know what to expect. If you own a business, you may at some point have to use personal assets for business purposes. I know your accountant may hate to hear that, but it's just the reality for some entrepreneurs. If you own a home, you know certain things must be maintained or replaced regularly. After a few years, roofs must be replaced, hot water tanks eventually burn out and, sometimes, driveways must be paved again. If you have children, eventually you may want to help them with their education. They only stay small for so long. Cars don't last forever. When you buy a car, you must consider the average life of that car. While layoffs may seem to come unexpectedly, there are also times when you can see economies start to slow down; especially if you work in industries like the automotive industry that can be very sensitive to global changes or consumer spending. These are red flags that you need to set money aside.

You must have an emergency fund. This fund should ideally cover three to six months of living expenses. Depending on the nature of your work and your household, this may need to extend beyond six months.

Advancing the Kingdom

We learned in the eighth chapter of Deuteronomy that God has a much bigger plan in place regarding the resources He allows us to manage. God's purpose for money is no different than anything else that God has created: to further the kingdom and bring Him glory. What makes money significant to this purpose is the fact that we can quantify what each dollar can achieve. Often, we can measure some of the fruit. Investing in the kingdom is no different from any other investment. You put money in it because you believe it will be profitable. You should have an expectation that it will be profitable. We put money into the kingdom of God, expecting to see growth, some sort of return or a profit. In God's eyes, the growth is spiritual maturity and discipleship. The return is saved souls. The profit is the fact that souls are ultimately saved. The better we are financially, the more we'll ultimately have to invest in godly initiatives. Even if you're not an investment expert, a 5% return on $100,000 is much more than 5% on $1,000. I know we can't always quantify things like this. But if you've served on any sort of church planning committee, you know how many programs must be reduced or eliminated due to lack of funding. There are no shortages of ministries dedicated to solving the world's problems, and investing to help today, and for generations to come.

Leaving an Inheritance

The thing I love about the Bible is the constant reminders that life is not about us and that everyone is affected by the decisions we make. Once we accept Jesus Christ as Lord, we're now laying down our lives for Christ, who ultimately suffered and gave Himself up for us. He went to the cross—not for Himself—but because we needed Him to go.

Think about it. When you made your last purchase, who did you think about? Did you consider someone else? Not only did Jesus model how to live practically, but he showed us many examples or what it means to sacrifice for others. If we're going to leave an inheritance, we must think beyond our own lives. We must think about the next generations and the ones who came before us. For many people, their parents or grandparents were laborers who may not have completed or obtained a formal education. They diligently saved and worked hard. They often sacrificed for their kids to go to college or start a business.

The parents who labored knew that if they sacrificed a larger house or nice car, their child would be the first to go to college. Not only did fathers sacrifice, but mothers did as well. In earlier years, it was unheard of for women to work outside of the home. The job of a mother is not only tiring and hard; it's the most important job. In the past, mothers often shelved their pursuit of formal education, amongst other things, for the greater benefit of the family. Today, many households contain both a mother and father who work. Everyone is in pursuit of The American Dream, but the American Dream often does not align with the Bible. We've seen generation after generation who not only doesn't know *how* to sacrifice, but *aren't willing to* sacrifice.

Proverbs 13:22 says, *A good man leaves an inheritance for his children's children, but the sinner's wealth is stored up for the righteous.* Did you notice the scripture says inheritance and not legacy? We have to pay close attention to not only the words used, but the context in which the words are used. The word legacy is one of the most overused words in our language today, especially as the conversations around money have increased. The Bible tells us to leave an inheritance for our children's children, not a legacy. According to the Merriam-Webster dictionary, a legacy can be anything transmitted or received from an ancestor or predecessor. As we leave this life, everyone will leave a legacy, good or bad; but not everyone will leave an inheritance, and that's what we are instructed to do. Let's not confuse legacy with inheritance. Even when we hear the word inheritance, it seems foreign to us because many have never seen anyone receive one, which is why we often view this term in a generic, theoretical sense. As we read Proverbs 13:22, our minds often go towards family values, ideas, work ethic and treatment of others. While all of these are important and vital to what we pass down to our children, that's not what this passage is referring to. The Hebrew word "naw-khal," which is used to describe inheritance, means "to distribute, divide, or cause to possess. How do we know the context or inheritance is referring to possessions, because the second part of the verse mentions the "sinner's wealth." We're not dividing an idea, nor are we leaving a portion of a value system. This Scripture is talking about possessions and land. The Scripture references a good man, not every man.

Again, the Scripture says that a good man leaves an inheritance to his grandchildren. Do you think about your grandchildren when you make financial decisions? When you're thinking about retirement, do you ever consider how that may impact your grandchildren? When you're considering purchasing a home or car, do you think about what this means for generations to come? Many of us don't think about our grandchildren until they get here or until they're of adult age. If you're in your 20s, 30s, 40s or even 50s, think about the grandchildren you don't have yet. If you're single, don't check out because this could be a niece, nephew or cousin. When we make financial decisions, we must understand that it doesn't just impact us.

Consider John who's 35 and married to Jennifer. Together, they have a son. John and Jennifer were both born into families that had horrible money habits. As a result, they didn't have much in the way of family help through college. Both had to take out student loans to pay for college, but they both have worked diligently to pay them off since graduation. Considering how serious they were about paying off their debt, John and Jennifer committed only to buy used cars. They didn't incur any additional debt while they were paying off their student loans. When John Jr. was born, they committed to make sure their children wouldn't have to incur the same financial struggles as they did. They started saving $50 per month from the day he was born. They invested this money at a conservative rate of 5% and, over the course of John Jr.'s life up through graduation from high school, they were able to accumulate $25,000. John Jr. received some partial scholarships to college. Coupled with the money his parents saved for him, he was able to go to college without incurring any debt. During the time they were saving, John and Jennifer also were able to save for retirement and purchase a home.

When John and Jennifer passed, John Jr. was 50. They not only left him $250,000 in cash and investments, but the home they owned was worth another $350,000. So, at the time of his parents' death, John Jr. had a total inheritance of $600,000. Keep in mind that John Jr. went through college without accruing any debt. When he graduated, he moved back with his parents since he was single after graduation. Over the course of five years, John Jr. stayed at home until he met his eventual wife. He was able to save and invest much of his money because he frankly didn't owe anyone. The only "debt" John Jr. even knew was the mortgage to his house, which of course he was able to pay off before he retired.

John Jr. married Sarah and had three kids. Keep in mind that, at age 50, John Jr. inherited $250,000 and a home worth $350,000. John Jr. and Sarah decided that since his parents' home was in great shape, and this was the house John Jr. grew up in, they would sell their current home and move into his parents' home. By now, John Jr. and Sarah have been married for 23 years. They are only seven years away from paying off their home. Needless to say, their house is worth a lot more today than it was 23 years ago. They also had two children who graduated from college and one more, who was preparing to enter college. At the time that John Jr. and Sarah sold their home, it was worth $200,000 and they owed $70,000 on their home. After commissions and closing costs, they made $120,000 profit on the home. They also had $250,000 in cash and investment they received in inheritance money—plus the money that John Jr. and Sarah saved on their own.

At the age of 50, they don't have a penny of debt, they have $250,000 in an inheritance, $500,000 of their own money saved, plus the home they received. They didn't need to use any of their inheritance, so they decided to give some to charities and invested the rest. Long story short, by the time John Jr. and Sarah passed, they were able to leave their three children an inheritance of $2,000,000.

If you're not like John Jr. and Sarah, who were born into some level of financial freedom and wisdom, it's okay because you have the power to change course today. I know this may seem like a story from an episode of *The Andy Griffith Show*, but I assure you it happens every day. But it doesn't happen overnight. If you don't find yourself in the place of John Jr., don't get discouraged or dismayed. That's literally the story of my life, as you probably picked up on in the preface of this book. I don't get angry about it, nor do I get mad at my parents. They did the best they could, considering the circumstances they were born into. Now, I have the opportunity to change the course of our family history. I'm not suggesting I'm John Jr., and my wife is Sarah; but our children and grandchildren will be in a much better position than where we started. Not from a sense of greed or worldly success, but they'll have a better jumpstart than we did. That's the underpinning theme in this passage: vision and sacrifice.

Did you see all those things in the story of John Sr.? First, he and his wife determined they wouldn't buy new cars, so they could pay off student loans and save for their children (vision and sacrifice). Secondly, when John Jr. received his inheritance, he didn't buy a new or bigger house. He did what they thought made the most financial sense and, because of their sacrifice, their children would start off much better than them. In addition, their grandchildren should be in an even better position than their parents. To make this Scripture come to life, someone must decide they will make financial decisions with future generations in mind, not just based on their own wants. Because Jack Jr. and his wife were already in a good financial position, they didn't have to spend the inheritance. This is the good side of things. Let's take a look at the other side.

Let's take a look again at John Sr. and Jennifer. What if they had made different choices? What if John Jr. was born to parents who lived the life that many wouldn't envy? A life where they found themselves living life too fast and were forced to deal with situations they couldn't handle?

Both of John Jr.'s parents worked, but they didn't save much. As they made money, they spent it just as fast. Because of this perpetual habit, they never found themselves in a position to give, let alone save money for John Jr. John Sr. finished high school and, during his senior year, found himself madly in love with his sweetheart, Jennifer. Jennifer and John Sr. quickly wed. But since neither one of their parents made provision for them, or taught them proper budgeting and saving habits, they found themselves head over hills in credit card debt throughout their marriage. To come up with the money to pay off their credit cards and vehicle loans, they had to remortgage their home several times. When they passed, the home wasn't paid off. Neither one of them purchased life insurance, so there was no money left to bury them or to pay off the home.

Out of the two stories, which one is more common in our society? Which story may be more common in our churches and family? Here's the gut check: If you died today, which story would be told of you? Would you be the first Jack Sr. or the latter? We hear these stories every day. We have the power to determine what the story of our families will be each day when we swipe our debit cards, charge a credit card or write a check. Good people can still make bad financial decisions that leave their families, churches and communities in worse shape. There's a bigger picture, even when our view may seem limited or dim. If a "good" person leaves an inheritance to their children's children, what type of person leaves their family with debt and nothing but grief?

Minor changes can drastically change the future, but you must have the heart to know you're not doing this for yourself. Far too many times, especially in the African-American dominated churches, we know people who have a Cadillac in the driveway, but no money in the bank. We have nice clothes, but no life insurance. We have the power to do things differently. We must prioritize what's most important and stick to it. There may be things that you want to do financially, but God doesn't allow you to. One of your heirs may be able to complete the journey and see the dream manifest that you started.

In 1 Chronicles 22, we see this exact situation with King David and his son, Solomon. David desired to build a new temple for the Lord. However, God determined David had killed too many people and had "too much blood" on his hands to build the temple. But, not his son Solomon. God told David that he couldn't complete the task, but that Solomon would. God told David that Solomon would experience peace, and not the war that David experienced. He didn't pout or get upset. Instead, he did what Proverbs instructs us to do. He set the resources and other provisions aside so that Solomon would complete the task. The chapter goes through all of the items David gathered for Solomon, and it specifically tells us David gathered these things in great quantities before his death. Solomon had more than enough resources to complete the temple, all because his father thought of him during his lifetime. I try to be careful not to add my own interpretation of Scripture, but maybe Solomon was able to write Proverbs 13:22 because he experienced his father leaving him an inheritance to help him in doing God's work.

If we take a look at the 6th chapter of Deuteronomy, we see Moses reminding the nation of Israel that God delivered them from slavery in Egypt, gave them these rules, statutes, and commandments to be set apart for him, and that they were to fear him and teach these things to future generations. The first half of verse 2 says, "that you may fear the Lord your God, your son, and your son's son." Don't miss that God's plan for us is to always think about the future generations. Throughout Scripture he calls Israel an inheritance for himself. We are called to be an inheritance, and leave an inheritance.

God Expects Us to Invest

If I'm going to lose the church, it's right here. Many Christians think investing is showing a love of money. This is where I get a lot of pushback. As we'll see in Ecclesiastes 11, investing is suggested for risk standpoints. But what if I told you that God expects us to grow our assets? Believe it or not, God expects us to invest our money. Let's go to Matthew 25:14-30. Just to give you a little background, this is a parable Jesus told his disciples in response to their question of how they would know the end of times. It's a parable, which means it uses metaphors, examples, and comparisons to make a greater point, but it still holds weight to our topic of stewardship.

> "For it will be like a man going on a journey, who called his servants and entrusted to them his property. To one he gave five talents, to another two, to another one, to each according to his ability. Then he went away. He who had received the five talents went at once and traded with them, and he made five talents more. So also he who had the two talents made two talents more. But he who had received the one talent went and dug in the ground and hid his master's money. Now after a long time the master of those servants came and settled accounts with them. And he who had received the five talents came forward, bringing five talents more, saying, and 'Master, you delivered to me five talents; here I have made five talents more.' His master said to him, 'Well done, good and faithful servant. You have been faithful over a little; I will set you over much. Enter into the joy of your master.' And he also who had the two talents came forward, saying, 'Master, you delivered to me two talents; here I have made two talents more.' His master said to him, 'Well done, good and faithful servant. You have been faithful over a little; I will set you over much. Enter into the joy of your master.' He also who had received the one talent came forward, saying, 'Master, I knew you to be a hard man, reaping where you did not sow, and gathering where you scattered no seed, so I was afraid, and I went and hid your talent in the ground. Here you have what is yours.' But his master answered him, 'You wicked and slothful servant! You knew that I reap where I have not sown and gather where I scattered no seed? Then you ought to have invested my money with the bankers, and at my coming I should have received what was my own with interest. So take the talent from him and give it to him who has the ten talents. For to everyone who has will more be given, and he will have an abundance. But from the one who has not, even what he has will be taken away. And cast the worthless servant into the outer darkness. In that place there will be weeping and gnashing of teeth.'"

I could write a short book on this passage alone. But, for the sake of your eyes and attention, I will do my best to unpack this Scripture as it relates to money. First, we must quantify what a talent is. During Jesus's lifetime, a talent was worth approximately 20 years of wages for a laborer. Today, if a laborer earned $40,000 per year, one talent would be approximately $800,000. I love the fact that, even though Jesus wasn't directly talking about money, he used the value of money to make a point. Whatever God gives us in the form of abilities, be it natural or financial, it has great worth to Him. Thus, it should have great worth to us. Whatever He gives is far more valuable than we realize.

In Matthew 25:15, He gave one five talents, another two and the last person, one talent, according to their abilities. This should create a sense of humility in all of us and free us from the tendency to perform like or compare ourselves to others. Whatever we have, God gave it to us according to our ability to manage it. That doesn't make us special though. We shouldn't poke our chests out, nor should we look down on others who have less. Also, for those who find themselves on the receiving end of the five talents, don't feel guilty about it—especially if you've been generous and faithful, and you've stewarded your talents well. If you find yourself with the two talents or even the one, you also must be careful not to compare yourself or covet the person with the five talents. God chose how He would distribute talents.

If many of us will be honest, many of us can't handle the five talents. No matter where we fall, God has given us all something and we should be thankful for that alone. Think about a time where you went out of your way to give someone something, only for them to not show any form of appreciation. Now imagine if that's what we did financially.

In the story, there were two servants who were good and one who was considered bad. The one with five talents brought back five more, and the one with two talents brought back two more. It's worth noting here that as Luke 12:48 says, "To whom much is given, much is required." God is much less concerned about the numbers as He is the activity. What made these two servants good was not the numerical value of what they brought back, but the point that they brought back more than what they were given. Each servant who was thought to be "good" was the one who produced more than what they were given. The other servant wasn't considered evil because he didn't bring back another two or five. God does not expect us to do the same as those who He's given more to. But, He does expect us to do something productive with whatever He gives us. The wicked servant knew what his master expected of him, yet he didn't do anything productive. He hid the talent out of fear. It seems that this servant didn't really know his master's heart. This is what's running rampant in the church today.

We know God wants us to honor Him, but we're not exactly sure how it relates to our money. We make decisions based on our misunderstanding of His expectations, as did this evil servant. Luckily, this is a parable that speaks directly to us about being good stewards of everything in this life. So, if you haven't been as faithful as you should with your finances, you're not going to hell. But, God isn't pleased when we don't do the best we can to honor Him financially.

Let's assume you have $100,000 to invest, and you presented it to an advisor to invest for you for a long-term investment. After 20, 30 or 40 years, they just give you back the original $100,000. Would you think they did a good job? Would you say that was a wise investment? Would you likely have some regret or level of disappointment? Think about it. God doesn't need us to do anything. He chooses to use us. What good would it do for God to give us something if all we're going to do is return to Him what He gave us in the first place? God expects us to produce increase with anything He gives us.

10 Practical Reasons to Invest

Wherever we are spiritually, will show up naturally, good or bad. Our motives, thoughts and responses are all a result of what will, or has already taken place spiritually. Handling our money is no different. We just touched on four primary ways that investing is supported biblically. If it's supported biblically, we need to do it practically. Let's review four reasons you *need* to invest your money.

1. Inflation
2. Retirement
3. Education
4. Inheritance

Inflation & Lifestyle

As an adult, there are certain purchases and/or expenses that we'll probably have for the rest of our lives. With improved technology, we've seen the prices of certain electronic devices go down. However, many of our expenses have increased over time, and this will continue. Think about the first time you mailed a letter. Do you recall how much a stamp cost? Now compare it to the price it is now. How much was gas the first time your parents let you drive the car? How about the price of your first home, or even basic goods, like eggs and milk? What we're dealing with here, my friend, is this good old thing called "inflation." Interestingly enough, due to the rapid increase in the cost of living during recent years, those collecting social security received the biggest increase in their benefits that we've seen over the past forty years. Inflation is often relative to goods and/or services, but the cost of living goes up somewhere every single year. As someone who has many clients who are retired and receiving social security, many of them saw prescriptions and medical premiums increase well above the increase in their social security benefits. For those who may be in apartments or condos, association fees and rent also increased.

According to the Social Security Administration (until recently), the cost of living has increased annually by 3.85% over the past 40 years, but during the six-year span of 2009-2015, the national average for a dozen eggs has gone from $1.77 to $2.75. These prices vary by geographic area, but this is an increase of approximately 55% on basic needs. The price of milk and groceries in general has significantly increased. I can't be the only one who feels they're spending more at the grocery store yet coming home with *less* food.

The largest expense for many retirees is medical, and it's not going down anytime soon. Medical costs are not only likely to go up over time, but it has become the hardest item to predict. Part of the reason medical costs have increased is because many people are living significantly longer than they were 50 years ago. Some of it may be technology, while some of it may just be that more people are more health conscious. The combination of the two has improved the lifestyle of some, but with older age sometimes comes the inevitable need for care. According to the Social Security Administration, a man who is 65 today can expect to live, on average, to age 84. A woman who is 65 can expect to live until age 87. Of this same age group, approximately 25% of 65-year-olds will live past 90, and 10% of them will live past 95. Clearly, women know something men don't. However, keep in mind that these are solely averages. While some may not make it to these ages, many will live well past them. Years ago, people could plan for a relatively short retirement of 15-20 years because people didn't live as long. Now people are living almost as many years in retirement that they spent working.

Everything we just mentioned has financial implications, so let's view all of these items from a budget standpoint. If what we've seen up to this point is true, it means every year that you're blessed to see another year, even if nothing drastically changes, it's going to cost you more money to meet your monthly needs.. Assuming we just add the average inflation percentage, what costs you $100 now costs $103.85 after just one year. Imagine what that looks like after 20 years. If your expenses are $55,000 a year, and these expenses increase by 3.85% per year, that $55,000 is now $167,000 per year after 20 years.

Now that we have some numbers to make things sensible, imagine if you're retired and this happens to you, but your source of income doesn't increase at the same rate. How do you get more money? It's been a long time since a bank account paid 4%, so investing is key to everyday living. I want to reiterate this because, many times, we view investing as being greedy or being too risky. However, if your expenses are consistently increasing, and your money stays the same, you run the risk of outliving your money. You can't afford to **not** invest.

In addition to inflation, you also must factor in your overall comfort and activities. I know the word "comfort" is taboo for Christians, and I don't mean it in the sense of feeling overly confident in a lifestyle or possessions. But there are things we enjoy and will likely want to continue over time. I'm an avid golfer, and this is a hobby that I want to continue. It can be an expensive gadget or technology that can help my game, and over time, equipment like golf clubs must be replaced. Whether your hobbies are fishing, hunting or sewing, all these things cost money. Even if your hobby is serving your local church or other non-profit organizations, not only does it cost you time—it costs you money. Though you may receive a credit on your income taxes, it costs money for you to drive where you serve. Serving does cost. Make sure you make provisions to do those things.

Retirement

This is the area where many people are already actively investing. How you plan here often has the most impact on all other areas. Since this is a very important area, I will spend a lot of time on retirement, but I will dedicate areas specifically to give you some planning resources to help plan your retirement. Remember, if you have assets that generate the income you need to live, you can consider retiring sooner than later.

Education

Education is one of those areas that may or may not be applicable to you, especially for those who don't have children, or your children are out of the house. Don't tune me out because there's someone who you may be able to assist in this journey with information. You may have a niece, nephew, cousin, sibling, parent or foundation that you would like to assist with educational funds. The million-dollar question is: Do I plan for retirement or education? The answer is, "Yes." Ideally, you should do both. If you can't save for both, save for retirement above a child's education. I know that may shock you but planning for retirement is more important. I know the ideal situation is to not have to borrow but, for many of us, loans are the only option when considering college. You can't borrow for retirement. There are far more options to pay for college than there are to get you through retirement. You will either receive social security, a pension, funds from investments or you'll continue to work. With that in mind, I want to give you some steps to help you prepare for educational planning before you even consider your educational planning investment options.

Very few things other than medical costs have increased in cost as much as tuition. So, the earlier you can start, the better. When I went to college, we didn't have $5 saved for it. I don't say that out of anger or disrespect to my family, but it's the reality of the situation. Even if you start late, whatever you do will be better than nothing. Your child will eventually appreciate it. As we review these tips, please keep an open mind. Everything we review is not necessarily monetary, but everything has a monetary value.

First, pay attention to your children's natural abilities and affinities. I know this can be difficult at times, but we have natural tendencies toward certain things. Those things need to be cultivated. It doesn't mean your children won't want to give up on these things at some point, but I think there's one thing or another that we've always loved to do that has shaped what we do now. There are likely some things that we wished we would have been pushed to learn or complete. God is the creator. We, as parents, are called to be cultivators of the creation, so they can freely create. We often make the mistake of trying to live vicariously through our children or pushing them to things we want them to do. Instead, we need to be prayerful about what God has created them to do. Remember, God is the creator, which means that God has already determined what He wants our children to become and accomplish. Ephesians 2:10 says *"For we are his workmanship created in Christ Jesus to do good words which he prepared beforehand, that we may walk in them."* While these good works are primarily focused on serving God and being a witness for Christ, I believe this scripture also accounts for what God has called our Children to do with their lives. God has already determined what He wants them to do, and it's our job to catch up to His plan.

As we often see, many people pursue careers in fields that are directly tied to their interests as children. This may allow your student to find a school that specializes in that field. Oftentimes, parents end up overpaying for school because students want to go to a popular school. Finding a school that specializes in a field of interest may not only open the door to go to a smaller school, but it may also open the door for scholarships. Another important aspect of choosing a school is the strength of the alumni network. Choosing a school that specializes in a field of study also opens the door for more impactful internships, which often turn into job placement.

For example, I never took much interest in school, outside of math. I enjoyed math because, even if you got the answer wrong, you had the opportunity to get "credit" for at least following the right methods. I liked the idea of that and the analytical aspects of math. When I was a teenager, my father told me I should consider the field of finance because of my love for math. He said, "You will always be able to find a job." I took all that in and went to Bowling Green State University because it was a smaller school, which is what I wanted. The school also has a reputable business program and strong alumni ties, in addition to affordable tuition. I declared finance as a major when I was a freshman and never changed it.

I know interests change, and I'm not condemning anyone who has changed their major. But many people change their major because they either gave up on their passion because it was difficult, or they didn't know what they wanted to do with that major. This often results in delayed graduation and more money spent, which brings me to another point. If you have a student who has no clue what they want to do as a career, they may not be ready to go to college. During my junior year of college, I was working as a fundraiser for the university and made contact with an alum who was an economics major. He worked for a major bank that was headquartered in my hometown. I told him my interests and while he told me he couldn't guarantee me anything, if I called him closer to graduation, he could get me an interview in his department. I took his phone number and called him the next year. He kept his word and got me the interview. Three days after graduation, I went to work for the same company. Through this same company, I met the person who gave me a shot at the position I wanted. The rest is history.

All of this happened because of the information I just shared, it wasn't because of me. Not only did all this happen, but I came out of school with a lot less debt than many of my peers. More importantly, I was able to find a position directly related to my degree.

    The second aspect of educational planning is estimating the cost of your child's education. As with anything else, it's hard to hit a target we're not aiming for. So, we first need to estimate what the cost of education will be. I emphasize education, not college, because your child's path may not be college. He or she may end up attending trade school, which still costs money. The thing about an estimate is just that; it's an estimate, so you can never guarantee that it will be 100% correct. However, at least you don't have to take shots in the dark. Full-court NBA shots have very low percentages. Some people have hit them, but no one hits them consistently. You want to be on the side that hits the mark at a higher rate and has a higher percentage of achievement. Many schools publish their historical tuition rates. It may take some leg work, but with financial calculators, you may be able to get a good estimate.

    To determine the total cost, take today's tuition rates at the university you desire for your student and determine what year your child will be in college. Then multiply that number by the historical annual increase in tuition for that school. Another option is to take the current cost of tuition and multiply it by the number of years your child will be in college by a general inflation rate. For example, if you have a 15-year-old student who will be in college in three years, you can take costs for the university and grow that number by the inflation rate you think makes sense. If your school costs $25,000 today, and we assume the costs of this school will increase by 5% per year, we can estimate that by the time our 15-year-old goes to school, the cost for school would roughly be $29,000.

    I want to take a step back and remind you that while everything we're discussing may not be relative right now, or at all in your life, as I'm always told, "Eat the meat and spit out the bones." If you're like me and your children are toddlers, you're probably unable to figure out a major and school for them right now. However, they may be eligible for a scholarship from your alma mater simply because you attended the school. Once you figure out the field of study, school and estimated costs, you can set more realistic goals. As with anything financial, there should be a goal attached to the end of your educational goal. You must consider what exactly you want to be able to do for your student. Do you want to pay for their education completely, or simply cover half the costs? Will you pay for graduate school only? Is your goal to cover just tuition, or do you want to also cover room and board, books and lab fees? You may also determine a flat dollar amount for your student, then work backwards to figure out what can be done. Let's say you hypothetically want to have $25,000 saved for education. Depending on the age of your student and how much of a return you expect on the money saved, you can determine with some confidence how much you must start saving now to reach the $25,000 mark by the time your student is off to college. Your financial goal may also be to do the same thing for each child, whether you save the same amount or pay for everything for each child. Either way, you can find a way to get closer to that number than you are today.

 The next step in planning for education is figuring out what's the best way to get you to your goal. Work with a professional, whether that's a financial advisor or a certified college planner. Planning on your own may cause you to fall victim to the deadly killer, analysis paralysis. Though this step will take much planning and thought, you don't want to overthink it to the point where you don't do anything. You can pay for education in many ways. It may take multiple avenues to get the job done. Ideally, you want to stay away from debt as much as possible. Outside of loans, you can always save through a general savings account or investment account specifically for higher education. You can always save the money in a bank account, but since those rates have historically been below inflation rates, and the fact that you must pay taxes on your interest, the bank may not be the best route to go. Another option is a general investment account. You can also contribute money to accounts like Coverdale educational savings account and 529 plans, which will be explained more in the investment options sections of the book.

The last option, and one that's often underutilized, is getting family involved. Think about all the times we see someone spend $25 on a toy, only for the child to play with the box. We see people spend the same amount of money on clothes that the kid will either wear out or outgrow. Either way, when you look back on your children's childhood, how much do you think is spent on toys and clothes? I'm not suggesting that your kids only play with boxes, nor am I suggesting your kids stay in a constant state of nakedness. I simply want you to look at things with the mindset of an investor. An investor looks at things and says, "Does this have the option of putting money back into my pocket?" I know some things are necessities, but I can only imagine how much we spend on things for our kids that add zero to their futures. In lieu of buying all toys and clothes for birthdays, graduations, baptisms and bar mitzvahs, make contributions to their education fund. Now, you must do this in a tactful way because we should appreciate whatever people are willing to do. So, please don't get offended if a Tickle Me Elmo still ends up in your home. I doubt that people will get mad at you for thinking about your child's education instead. For some grandparents, and other relatives in the family, this could be another estate planning tool for those who want to give to their heirs, but still have some control over the funds. If you have a taxable estate that you need to make non-taxable, talk to your CPA and financial advisor to determine how you can use education to do that.

Not only can professionals give you options for self-funding your student's education, but they can also help you maximize any financial aid eligible benefits. They may have access to scholarships you're not familiar with. It's often said that millions of dollars of scholarship opportunities go unclaimed each year, which seems almost impossible when you consider how many students must borrow money for college.

Of course, there are eligibility requirements to scholarships, but you also must consider if the issue is familiarity versus eligibility. Your financial professional may not only be able to point your student to lower cost options for school, but they may know of a scholarship that directly works with your student's goals. I haven't personally used it, but you can also look into www.scholly.com, which is a website and app that allows you to search and locate many scholarships you may not be familiar with. The bottom line is not to overthink things, but to know your options. Seek a professional and get to work. You pay for college the same way you eat your favorite foods: one bite at a time.

Leaving an Inheritance

Leaving an inheritance is by far one of the most neglected areas of financial management for all people. This shouldn't be the case for Christians, and I don't say this from a superiority complex. But the fact that we're instructed several times throughout Scripture to think of the future is more than confirmation. Proverbs 13:22 says, *A good man leaves an inheritance to his children's children, but the sinner's wealth is stored up for the righteous.* This again admonishes us to think about, not only our futures, but our grandchildren's future. Always start with the end goal in mind. So, even if you don't have any grandchildren, you still want to think about if something happened to you, what would you want your family to say? What would you want your family, friends, community or church to have to further the work of God? At the heart of any inheritance planning must be selflessness. But unfortunately, in our microwave "me-centered" culture, we've been taught to do whatever we feel. We don't realize we may be ransoming our children's futures in the process. Whether we realize it or not, when we leave here, we will leave someone something. It's a matter of what.

SECTION II

Understanding Investments

11 Investment Options

As we've discussed, there are multiple reasons why you want to invest, but as we invest we must remember to diversify our assets. Some would lead you to believe this concept of diversification started on Wall Street, but look in the bible. Ecclesiastes 11:1-2 (NIV) says. "Ship your grain across the sea; after many days you **may** receive a return. Invest in seven ventures, yes, in eight; you do not know what disaster may come upon the land." Make sure you aren't relying on one thing financially because that one thing can be taken away. But we also must remember that God has made an investment in us and He expects a return on that investment. So, it's up to us to use wisdom in the area of investing. Many times, we want to know how to invest. But I wanted to make sure I explained the "why" before the "how" because when the "why" is absent, the "how" can become worldly and turn into greed, which is what we want to keep away from. We will explore some of your investment options. We'll start with the most basic and work our way up to the more complex.

Some of the following items you may argue aren't investments, but I want to use the word investment in its most basic form, which is the outlay of money for income or profit. Basically, anything that you put your money in, and expect some sort of return, can be viewed as an investment. That's how I would like you to view it, not just placing money in the stock market.

I want to continue to emphasize that investing should keep your end goals in mind and may look something like this:
- Investing in Mutual Fund A is the best option to achieve your goal

- Investing in stock B provides needed cash flow for retirement income needs

- Investing in a Certificate of Deposit aligns with your time frame and risk tolerance

As you can see, whatever you do needs to have a reason "why" and a goal attached to it. For now, don't worry about the actual investment mentioned above, and focus on the concept. We will come back to the actual terms and how these things work. We don't invest in anything just because we've heard it's the right thing to do or it will make us (X) amount of dollars. We do it because it's the best fit for our individual needs. The information you're receiving is meant simply to enlighten and encourage you to take some steps now. But to do what's right for you, work with a financial advisor. It's very dangerous to give blanket advice, especially when it comes to investments and life insurance. A doctor wouldn't dare write you a prescription without first knowing what you're allergic to and what you may be already taking. The wrong mixture of drugs can be deadly, and the same is true financially. No one should give you investment advice without completely knowing your situation.

Bank Instruments

Bank instruments are typically going to be your most basic investment for short-term needs. As of late, there have been alternative investments that banks and credit unions offer, but they're not risk-free. Risk, at its basic level, means the chance of an adverse or undesired event is present. If I throw a party outside, there's a risk that it can rain and ruin the party. Risk, from an investment standpoint, is often defined as the chance that you can lose money. But when you consider risk, we must define what risk means to you and evaluate the greatest risk you face. Risk, for some, may mean the chances of losing money are present. While, to others, risk may refer to running out of money. No matter where you are, and where you want to be financially, to get there, you need to establish a savings account. Check with your financial institution to make sure you adhere to minimum deposits and other requirements to maintain a free account. However, don't leave money in your checking account for safety and growth reasons. Use your checking for everyday items like bill payments and grocery shopping. Money that you consider saving should not be kept in your checking account. Remember your budget and the goals you've set for yourself. Place those dollars where they belong.

Money Market Accounts

A money market account is often just a fancy name for a type of savings account, which either offers a higher rate of return and/or requires a larger balance. Many banks and credit unions offer the money market account to entice their customers to keep larger amounts in the bank. They offer them at a more competitive rate than one would receive on a checking or savings account. Some institutions set standards that require you to maintain an amount of money in the account at all times. You may also have to limit the amount of withdrawals you can take per month. The money market is a place where you can keep money that you need to access quickly. Whether it's your emergency fund, or money you're putting aside for an upcoming car purchase, the money market is where you place money you may need right away. In an ideal situation, this account continues to grow by deposits and interest. Even as things come up, such as a flat tire, this is money you may or may not need in the near future. Never use this money for anything other than its intended purpose.

There may be times where you realize you have too much money in your money market account. In that case, consider investing in other places. What's "too much money"? Let's say you're in a stable work environment (if there's such a thing anymore). You know it costs you $4,000 to live each month. Assume the perfect scenario, where you don't have any debt and your car is relatively new. So, you won't need to purchase a car anytime soon. You've managed to save well, and you've accumulated $75,000 in your money market account. Hypothetically, you only need to have $12,000-$24,000 (3-6 months expenses) in case of job loss or an emergency. You can take the "extra" $50,000 in your money market account and invest in options that offer higher returns. This is the exact scenario where some people are and, every six months, they move money around. As you consider money market accounts, keep in mind that some of them offer promotional rates for a specific amount of time. Pay attention to your rate and make sure you understand the withdrawal privileges and balance requirements to avoid any fees. If you find yourself in a scenario where you can't fulfill the requirements, visit your financial institution to change your account. With the increase in government bonds and bills, money markets and certificates of deposits have become popular options again.

CDs

Certificates of deposits are called time deposits because they require you to place your money in an account for a specific time frame. The time frame is an agreement between you and your bank or credit union. You agree to leave your money in the account for a predetermined amount of time, and the bank agrees to pay you an amount of interest over that time frame.

Let's assume you have $10,000 that you're willing to invest for two years. Your local bank may offer you 4.25% each year for that two-year period for keeping your money in the certificate for the period of time. When you buy a CD, the bank is essentially using your money to lend out to other people who want to buy a home, car or pay off debt. The interest they charge versus the interest they pay you is one of the ways they make their money. Again, if they're paying you 4.25%, but they're charging me 7% on my mortgage, the bank is essentially earning a 2.75% return. It's likely less due to expenses, but you get the point.

There are a few things to consider before you purchase a CD. First, ask yourself, "What is this money for?" Anytime you purchase a CD, you should have a matching goal across the same period of time the CD will last. If you buy a two-year CD, buy it with a two-year goal in mind. If you plan on buying a house in three years, consider buying a three-year CD if the rate is worth the while. Many people buy CDs because they view them as "safe." The problem with the thought process is once you factor in the increase in cost of living and income taxes paid on CD interest, you may lose money. If you have a four-year CD paying 4%, but you're in a 25% tax bracket, and the cost of living has gone up 3.2% (according to The Social Security Administration 2023,) you lost ⅕ of a percent (4%-1% in taxes-3.2% inflation.)

Another issue with CDs is the fact that there may be other investment options that pay a higher rate for the same given time frame or longer. There have been several occasions where I've found money market rates higher than CD rates. Though you can typically draw out your interest on your CD, if an emergency comes up and you need to close it early, you may have to pay a penalty, which could result in you receiving less money than you originally invested. It's important to remember that if you decide to purchase a CD, make sure it fits with the specific time frame that you have plans for the money. Also, make sure you visit the bank each time it matures. Certificates of deposits should never be allowed to roll over on their own because when your CD matures, it's credited with current interest rates, which are often lower than where you started. This is called reinvestment risk. Again, if you buy a CD, make sure you won't need the money prior to maturity. Once you consider taxes and inflation, CDs may not be the best long-term investment solution. CD time frames can vary from 30 days to 10 years, so make sure you do your research. Like your money markets, CDs may also have minimum balances, which can range from $500-$25,000. Like money markets, financial institutions around you are typically running promotions for CDs. So, just keep your eyes open and stay on top of the maturity dates of your CD's.

Market Linked CDs

Market linked certificates of deposit are newer to the market but have been gaining a lot of ground for banks and other financial institutions lately. A market linked CD is a time deposit that's "linked" to a group of stocks, or an index, such as the S&P 500 or Russell 2000. The objective of purchasing a market linked CD is to have the opportunity to earn higher returns than what you would typically find on a regular bank CD, while still providing safety of your money. Historically, investments that are linked to the stock market have outperformed bank interest rates. However, your return in a market linked CD is not guaranteed, which is a major difference between typical CDs. One similarity between regular CDs is the guarantee of your initial investment if you hold it until maturity.

With a market linked CD, you will see the value of your CD move up and down with the investments it's linked to, but the principal is FDIC-insured through whatever bank issues the CD. They also have options for those who are looking for income and those who look for growth, or a combination of the two. Many of them also will guarantee a return of principal if the account owner dies before maturity and the CD is worth less.

By now, you may be thinking, "This sounds too good to be true." It's not. But, you must understand the components of the CD you may consider purchasing. Some of the CDs that are linked to a basket of stocks have caps on them, which limits how much you can make. This is one of the things you give up in return for the safety of your initial investment. For instance, though this group of stocks may perform 10% per year, you may only be allowed to make 6% per year. Not to suggest these are bad investments, but if you end up with a portfolio of underperforming stock, your possible return could get pulled down to the point where you make little to no money. On the other side of the coin, you may get a basket of stocks that perform well and receive returns higher than what a normal bank CD over that same time may have returned. I've seen both sides of the coin. With many investments, there's an uncertainty of whether you'll make a profit. But the capped rate of return on these market linked CDs are your trade-off for the safety of your investment.

The growth market linked CDs as described are typically based on standard benchmark indexes, such as the S&P 500. However, many of them are based on a portfolio that is professionally managed by the bank that issues the CDs. These portfolios are typically designed to keep the ups and downs of investing to a minimum, while presenting the opportunity for upside gains. The CD issuer will decide when and where to make portfolio changes. You would just hold the CD and trust their expertise and knowledge to manage the assets. One thing to consider with these growth CDs is that they may not pay you until the certificate matures (5, 6 or 7 years). As an incentive, some of the issuers will offer you full participation of whatever the portfolio makes from start to finish or, in some cases above the portfolio.

For instance, I've seen offers in the past where investors in the CDs were offered twice the total return at maturity. Let's assume you bought a five-year CD that achieved 5% per year (ignoring compounding) or 25% total return. In a 200% offer, you would make 50% (2 x 25%), or an average rate of return of 10% per year. In a 125% offer, your final payout would be 31.25% (1.25 x 25), or 6.25% per year. These CDs aren't your normal bank CDs. There are different dynamics to understand.

Though the issuer of the certificate may offer the opportunity to sell your CD early, they are not required to. So, make sure whatever funds you allocate to a market linked CD are funds you won't need over the life of the CD. Many of the issuers will allow beneficiaries to receive at least the original investment if the account owner dies before maturity. But, if you do decide to sell the CD before maturity, there may be a penalty. Market conditions could also result in you getting less than what you originally invested. Again, your original investment is only guaranteed if you hold the CD until maturity. Another aspect to consider is that these markets linked CDs still fall under the FDIC limits of $250,000. So, be aware of how much money you have with any individual bank. Like most investments, market linked CDs cannot guarantee a return. However, they allow you to invest without risking your initial investment . There's always the risk that you don't make any money, but leaving it dormant in a bank account almost guarantees you don't make a return on your money.

When purchasing CDs, you must also consider the taxes. The interest earned on CDs are taxed at your ordinary income rates each year, which may be higher than capital gain taxes on things like stocks and mutual funds. It may not be advantageous for you, unless the CD is in a retirement account. The growth CDs are taxed differently. A small portion of taxes are payable each year and taxed as ordinary income, even though you haven't received any profit other than what's possibly on your investment statement. However, because of regulation, you typically must purchase them through a licensed financial advisor. It's important that you seek the help of a professional advisor to fully understand if a market linked CD fits into your financial plan.

Bonds

Bank investments are FDIC-insured by the federal government, so they are typically viewed as the safest. Now we will move up the risk ladder to view bonds. The world of investments has changed quite a bit over the years. So, no matter what you may pick up from this book, this is a simplified version of your investment options. You'll still need to seek a professional financial advisor.

Bonds are typically called debt instruments because they usually involve some borrowing of funds, with the promise to pay it back later. When you take out a mortgage to buy a home, you're borrowing the money from the bank with the promise that you will pay them back over several years. The risk with the bank allowing you to borrow the money is the fact that you may not pay it all back—or any of it back. To assume this risk, and to compensate them for borrowing their money, the bank charges you interest. In some cases, the bank will either require you to buy mortgage insurance or they will buy it from another company. The interest payment could be a combination of risk and opportunity cost because, if the bank allows you to borrow $250,000 for your home, that's $250,000 that they've lost the opportunity to utilize for other ventures.

When you, as an investor, purchase a bond, whomever you purchase your bond through is the borrower. You are the creditor. I know that may seem weird or backwards, but the roles reverse when you buy a bond versus a home. Not to confuse you, but there are some fundamental differences between mortgages and bonds. We will unpack them here. Assume J.P. Morgan Chase wants to build a new facility. Instead of using their own money, they would rather borrow the funds for the project. As an investor or buyer of one of their bonds, Chase is essentially telling you that if you allow them to borrow your money, not only will they pay you interest for borrowing your money, but they will return your money to you over a period of time. What makes bonds unique is, even though the value of the bond will go up and down throughout the time you own it, typically the amount of interest you receive doesn't change. This is why so many retirees favor bonds.

Assume you purchase a ten-year bond from J.P. Morgan Chase that pays 4% for $100,000. You will receive $4,000 in interest payments each year, which you can use to pay bills, for vacation or to give to charity. Interest payments from individual bonds cannot be reinvested, so it either sits in the account, or it gets sent to you as income. Let's assume that the second year, your bond hasn't performed as well. Now, your $100,000 bond is now worth $97,500, but your interest payments are based on your original investment. So, you still get $4,000 a year in interest, despite the decline in value. But if your bond goes up to

$105,000, your interest payments still would be based on the original $100,000 investment.

Under normal market conditions, the issuer of the bond will return money back to you. In our example above, let's assume your ten-year bond is at nine years, 11 months and 30 days. It's set to mature in a couple of days, but market conditions have been rough, and your investment is worth $85,000. Keep in mind you still received $4,000 in interest each year. Once you reach the ten-year mark, not only will you receive your last interest payment; but your full $100,000 will be returned to you, despite the recent 15% in market decline you've experienced. Bonds also trade in the open market. So, though your bond has a time frame attached to it, under normal market conditions, you may be able to sell your bond early. But you would get what it's worth and what someone is willing to pay for your bond.

As you approach bonds, it's important to know that basic bonds fall into one of three categories: government bonds, municipal (muni) bonds and corps (corporate bonds). I also listed them based on their risk, from lowest to highest.

Government bonds are considered to be the safest bonds because they are backed by the full faith of the United States Government. In order for an investor not to receive their money back from a government bond, the U.S. would essentially have to be in ruins and unable to meet their obligations as a country. Government bonds are used in monetary policies, foreign trade, mutual funds, life insurance, annuities and pension plans. Because government bonds are guaranteed to be paid, the interest rate tends to be lower than other bonds. They're considered very low risk, or in many cases a risk-free asset. In very low interest rate environments, you may see the interest on these bonds to be unacceptable for your portfolio. Your thoughts on the state of the U.S. will truly determine how "safe" you believe government bonds to be. But the risk of not receiving interest payments and/or not receiving your money back at maturity is going to be the lowest amongst the bond family. Because the interest rates may be lower in government bonds, one of the incentives of buying a government bond is that the interest received from the bond is tax-free on the federal level.

As we take a step up on the bond ladder, we move into municipal bonds. Muni bonds are typically issued by various non-profits or local divisions of states throughout the U.S. for various reasons. Where federal bonds are guaranteed by the U.S. government, muni bonds are often backed on state and city levels. Although some of the bonds may be insured, there is a greater risk that the issuer could fail to make interest payments (as compared to government bonds) and/or return your money to you at maturity. Municipal bonds can be issued from universities that want to expand their facilities on campus, a local city that wants to build a new library, a local city that wants to revamp their water and sewage systems, or a local hospital that wants to build a new facility. As you can see, municipal bonds can cover many types of projects across the U.S. It's important to not only be familiar with the locality of where the bond is issued, but also what type of muni bond your potential investment may fall under.

There are various aspects you must consider when buying a muni bond. You can make the choice to stay within your state or buy them nationwide. One of the incentives when purchasing muni bonds from the state where you live is the fact that interest from those bonds are income tax-free on a federal, state and local level. If you buy a bond outside of your home state, the tax-free interest is only at the federal level. You may be thinking, "Why would I go outside my home state?" On the surface, one of the reasons might be simple diversification. Although I was born and raised in Cleveland, Ohio and lived in Detroit, MI for 15 years, I may want to diversify outside of these states for different opportunities. This isn't uncommon. But if you are going to consider this type of strategy, make sure you work with an advisor and/or investment company that has experience purchasing bonds throughout the U.S. and its territories. Even that experience doesn't guarantee your results will be positive.

One of the major scares of the past few years has been bonds issued from Puerto Rico. Since Puerto Rico is a U.S. territory, bonds from there are considered municipal bonds. Unfortunately, their economy has not grown anywhere close to the point of expectations. Many of their bonds defaulted, causing investors to suffer large losses. If you're going to purchase muni bonds, like any other investment, make sure you understand what you're purchasing. This is a very simplified view of municipal bonds. There are other considerations to the equation. But, hopefully, you feel more empowered to know what questions to ask if you're presented with a municipal bond.

Lastly, as we move to the top of the risk ladder concerning bonds, we have our normal corporate bonds. Corporate bonds, or corps, are exactly as they sound: bonds that are issued from corporations. These corporations will range in both size and industry. But if you talk to an advisor or a bond trader, they'll show you that many of the companies you're currently buying goods from have either issued bonds in the past or are still issuing bonds today. The reason corporate bonds are viewed as the riskiest out of the three is the fact that no government or state entity is backing those bonds. Your guarantee of interest payments, and the return of your money, is solely based on the strength of the company you're buying the bond from.

Let's assume Ford Motor Company continues to sell F-150 trucks at such a rapid rate that they need to build a new facility. Ford can issue a bond to raise the money to build the plant. They will then repay the bond through projected increase in sales. Clearly, Ford is backing this bond. So, if they were to get into financial trouble, there would be a greater risk of loss than you would find in a government or municipal bond. If a corporation like Ford were to get into financial trouble, or experience bankruptcy, bondholders receive payment prior to stockholders because the bondholders are considered creditors. Stockholders are considered owners. In bankruptcy, any distribution of assets is given to creditors before owners. Depending on what type of bond you hold, you may be first in line. But this, of course, assumes there are assets left to divvy up.

Corporate bonds don't typically offer any tax benefits, unless they are held inside of retirement accounts. So, when you receive interest from them, you are taxed. When you couple that with increased risk, it's common that you may find corporate bond rates are higher than government or municipal bonds. Bonds can be very simple or complex, and each type of bond carries its own form of risk. However, the degree of exposure to these different risks will vary. For our discussion, we'll focus on credit/default risk and reinvestment risk.

Default risk is arguably the most important risk to consider prior to making a bond purchase because, no matter how much income it may produce, if there's a heightened risk, the issuer may not meet its obligations. Then, the higher interest payment becomes irrelevant. One thing you can use to help determine default risk is the credit rating of the bond issuer. There was big news a few years ago that sent ripples through world economies and created some fluctuation in the stock market. That was when the United States lost its AAA credit rating from Standard & Poor's.

Standard & Poor's, along with Moody, Fitch and A.M. Best are the most notable names that issue these credit ratings. They all have their own ranking systems for what various letter and number combinations suggest. When a company, municipality or government agency receives a AAA, it suggests there's a small likelihood that default would take place and these entities have "superior" financial strength. So, when the U.S. credit ratings were lowered, it suggested around the world that we weren't in as good of financial shape that we had been in years prior. The risk for default was now heightened. It still doesn't mean default will happen, but I don't know any circumstance where something being viewed as weaker or weakened was a good thing. Make sure you understand, not only where they are as far as their credit ratings, but also how long they've had that rating. How long has the company been in business? These pieces of information can usually be found on the company's website under the "financial" information. The age of a company, like everything else, shouldn't be the sole reason you choose to invest in a company. We've seen older companies go into bankruptcy, too. I believe it's important to look at the various economic and political changes that companies have been through. But, on the flipside, I wouldn't be easily dismissive of newer companies, either.

Additionally, reinvestment risk is another aspect to consider when investing in bonds. Reinvestment risk comes in two forms on bond issues: the interest payments and the maturity of the bonds. Remember, the interest from individual bonds is typically fixed and can't be reinvested. You receive those interest payments, and, at maturity, the bond issuer is returning your money to you. Whether it's the return of your investment, or your interest payment, you have a decision to make: "What do I do with this money?" Many times, the interest payments from bonds are used to supplement income or pay specific expenses. However, some people let their interest payments accumulate in a bank account. As those interest payments are building, you may decide to reinvest them in other options. Reinvestment risk comes up because you may not be able to invest those interest payments into investments that pay the same return you received on your bond. Suppose you still have your 25-year bond at 4%. After five years, you decide to start using the interest payments to buy shares of another investment. But this new investment is paying less than what you're receiving on your bond. Let's say you put $100,000 into this bond, and you are receiving $4,000 a year in interest payments. There's another investment you want to purchase, but it requires a minimum investment of $20,000. As the money is accumulating, the bank account that holds the interest payments isn't paying as much interest as the bond is. Now that you've saved up enough money to buy the $20,000 investment, the returns on those have also lowered. The same happens when your five-year bond matures. If interest rates on new bonds are lower, you can't find a comparable replacement. Some bonds also have call features, where bonds can be redeemed early at the discretion of the bond issuer if certain conditions are met. This is the gist of reinvestment risk, which must be considered if you're purchasing individual bonds.

For years, bonds have been "sold" as being safe investments. Though they typically do carry less risk than stocks, they do have their own set of risks. So, make sure you do your due diligence. Prior to purchasing an individual bond, consider the company/agency; how long they've been in business; the line of business the company is in; their credit ratings; the length of the bond; the purpose behind investing in the bond and current interest rate environment.

Annuities

Whether it's in face-to-face meetings with people, or during group presentations, the most questions I receive are regarding annuities. As a matter of fact, if I was a betting man, I would place a bet that if you're already planning your retirement, or are currently living in retirement, the sight of the word "annuity" brought some emotion to the forefront. It could be excitement, but from my professional experience, it's usually a bunch of question marks or just a flat-out turn-off.

Annuities are investments that can be as simple or as complex as they desire to be. Many times, people have only heard bits and pieces of what they are and how they work, even if they currently own annuities. On its most basic level, an annuity is a contract between you and an insurance company. You're typically committing your investment dollars to a specific amount and time frame, and the annuity company is offering you some type of guarantee in the form of safety, income, interest rate returns or inheritance benefit. In many instances, they offer income. Though some people use annuities for different reasons, the basic function of an annuity is to offer lifetime income to an investor. Over time, annuities have been offered with many bells and whistles that, on some levels, have complicated the understanding of what they are and how they work. Annuities come in different forms, depending on your needs. Many times, they are used in connection with retirement planning. You'll soon see why. I will focus on the four most common types. Any other form will be an extension of one of the four: an income annuity, fixed annuity, fixed indexed annuity, or a variable annuity.

Income Annuity

An income annuity is a vehicle that allows you to place a lump sum or pay over time into a contract with the insurance company. They pay you a set amount of income, which often can be received for at least your lifetime. The idea behind the income annuity is to ultimately create your own pension funds. The amount of income you will receive typically depends on the amount you invest, your age and withdrawal options The idea behind an income annuity is to make sure you don't outlive a specific amount of money (what you invest), or it could be to simply invest a particular amount of money to make up for a gap in your income needs.

Income annuities have changed over the years. But, many times when you purchase one, you're expecting to receive the income within a year. Some will allow you to start accumulating in earlier years and receive income later, which is how your basic pension works. The amount you receive also depends on whether the payments can continue to a beneficiary. In income annuities, there are standard payment options, such as life-only, life with period certain, and joint with rights of survivorship. Life-only is typically going to be your highest payout because it will only pay, as its title states, for one life only. The insurance companies have people much smarter than me to calculate someone's life expectancy and they base their payments on that. Under life-only, since it's only one person's life, it becomes easier to calculate on the insurance company's end.

If you were to elect a life-only payment option, it's vital that you understand that once the person who receives the payments dies, all payments stop, even if there were funds left over in the account. Suppose someone invested $100,000 into an annuity that pays $7,000 per year in income. The person was scheduled to receive that for life. If this person receives payments for 10 years, then dies, that $30,000 left over ($100,000 investment - $70,000 income payments) stays with the insurance company. I know this thought may outrage you, which is why you must make sure you understand what you're doing. There are some strategies where a life-only payment option makes sense, but that may not be the case for you. This is very important to understand because people will unknowingly make a "life-only" option for their pension from their job, and mistakenly leave their surviving spouse without any survivor income.

Investments always have risk, and one of the major risks associated with retirement planning is running out of money. The insurance company is also taking a risk because if you live longer than they expect, you may start receiving income on their dime. Suppose you are the purchaser of a $100,000 annuity, paying $7,000 per year. After 20 years of receiving payments, you're still alive and well. Even if you assume a rate of interest along the way, you've received $140,000 in payments and only invested $100,000. Another aspect that will impact your interest payments is if you choose to take smaller payments up front, so you can receive increases over time. The cost of living goes up every year. A fixed income payment over the next 10 or 20 years could be dangerous.

Under life with period certain, payments would still be received for life for the primary person. Income may continue to a beneficiary if the account owner dies within the "period certain" time frame. Let's assume an investor purchases an annuity for $100,000 that pays the same $7,000 each year under a life with 15 years period certain. That means the primary person would receive payments for life. But, if they died within that 15 years, their beneficiary would receive payments until the 15 years are up. If the primary person receives their payments for 10 years and dies, the beneficiary can expect to receive the $7,000 in payments for the remaining five years, or $35,000 in total payments. Even if there's money still left in the contract, the beneficiary can only expect payments for the remainder of the period. So even in our same example of a 15-year period certain annuity, if the account owner dies at year 14, the beneficiary would only receive payments for a year.

It's also important to understand that if the primary person lives beyond the period certain time frame, no survivor benefits will be paid. Instead of a 15-year period certain, let's assume you have $100,000 invested that pays $4,000 for life, with 20 years period certain, and the primary person dies at year 22. A total of $88,000 in payments has been received out of the $100,000. Even though $12,000 was technically still in the contract, that money is not passed on to heirs. Life-only and period certain annuities are most notably used if someone doesn't have a spouse or kids, or if they will use the income for other investment or insurance reasons.

Joint with Rights of Survivorship (JTWROS)

This is yet another investment strategy where the titles give you the overarching understanding of what it means. Much of the time, a JTWROS option is chosen by married couples who want to receive income for both lives. That's exactly what this payment option will provide. As I previously mentioned, and you've probably figured out on your own, JTWROS will typically pay the lowest amount of income because the longevity risk for the insurance company is far greater. Imagine you have a married couple who are both 70 at the time of the first income payments. They continue for 10 years and the husband dies (Sorry, fellas. It's just the norm). But the surviving wife lives another 15 years beyond her husband's death. The insurance company has now paid out money for 25 years, where their original estimates may have been for 20 years between the couple. Though this payment option is the lowest, if a couple is concerned about their spouse (as I hope you would be), especially in circumstances where a spouse doesn't have a pension, this may be a feasible option for some of your assets. For those who do have pensions, you may have noticed that these are basically the same options for many pension plans. If you haven't got to the point where you've made this election, you will if you have a pension. Most of the income annuity and pension plan options can't be changed once the election is made. So, it's very important that you work with a professional who understands your needs.

Fixed Deferred Annuity

Although every annuity offers a feature called annuitization that turns the annuity into an income annuity, fixed deferred annuities are often used for people who are still in the accumulation phase of saving for retirement. You probably have noticed my pattern of the use of words like "often" and "typically" because there are always alternative ways and reasons to use an investment. I'm not suggesting that going off script is wrong, but I will explain things based on the objective of the product design. As it relates to fixed annuities, they typically fall on the low end of the risk ladder. The insurance company that you buy the annuity from typically has reserve requirements that call for the insurance company to have adequate money set aside to pay their fixed annuity holders should financial difficulty arise. As a matter of fact, some insurance companies not only have reserves large enough to meet all their obligations, but some keep extra funds on top of the reserves. Fixed deferred annuities can range anywhere from three years to 20 years. The amount of interest you receive will be based on the amount you invest, the interest rate environment, the length of the contract, and the interest rate option selected.

One of the features you will also find on fixed deferred annuities is a guaranteed minimum interest rate, which kicks in after the guaranteed period of your annuity. Let's look at an example so we don't get lost in definitions.

Suppose you purchase a five-year annuity that guarantees 2.5% for the first three years and guarantees the rate won't go below 1.5% for the remainder of the contract. This guaranteed minimum ensures you that if interest rates get very low (as they are now), you will have a bare minimum return. Both the guaranteed rates and the minimum rates will usually follow the move of the overall interest rate environment. So, when interest rates on bank accounts and mortgages are higher, you may find annuity rates are higher. When they are lower, you can expect the annuity rates to be the same because, many times, they are partly based on government bond yields.

Another aspect of a fixed annuity is the tax deferred component of the annuity, which allows you to defer taxes until retirement, even though the funds you invest may not be in a retirement account. If you are 50 and pull $50,000 from a savings account, and invest in an annuity, you don't have to claim the interest on your taxes until you withdraw the funds in retirement. If the money is from a 401K rollover, or an IRA that money is already tax deferred, it doesn't get any additional special tax treatment. The tax deferral alone is the reason why some people buy annuities to shield money they aren't using from income taxes until they presume to be in lower tax brackets in retirement. One thing to note about deferred annuities is if you invest in them, unless you're taking special withdrawals, the money can't be withdrawn until 59 ½. It's important to know that withdrawals from an annuity are taxed as earnings first, and typically if you withdraw more than the company allows you will often pay large fees.

Fixed Indexed Annuities

Fixed indexed annuities are like a fixed annuity, but the difference is that the annuity offers an "indexed" function that provides for the opportunity to receive higher returns on your money. It's one of the "safer" ways you will find to seek higher returns. Keep in mind that safety is based on the financial strength of the insurance company you buy the annuity through. The indexed annuity typically has multiple "buckets" you can place your money in within the same annuity contract. The simplest bucket is the fixed portion that functions just like the fixed deferred annuity that we just reviewed. This bucket receives a "fixed rate" of interest that may be the same for multiple years or change from year to year. Nonetheless, you'll know ahead of time what that "bucket" pays.

The "indexed" portion of the annuity is usually tied to common benchmarks like the S&P 500, NASDAQ, EAFE and Russell 2000. As of late, more annuity companies are offering more options tied to professionally managed portfolios. The idea behind the indexed bucket is the opportunity to make higher returns based on the performance of the index, without taking the risk of actually investing directly in these indexes. As long as you don't break your contract, the index annuity guarantees you won't lose your money if the index goes down. To compensate for the safety portion of the annuity, your upside is often "capped." A typical index bucket looks like this: You can make up to 5% if the S&P 500 goes up. But if it goes down, you won't lose money. You just wouldn't earn anything in the indexed bucket that year. Let's assume your cap rate stays at 5% for five years. Here's how your returns would look:

Year 1. S&P 500: 10%. You make 5% (Max Cap Rate).

Year 2. S&P 500: 3.5%. You make 3.5% (100% growth up to the cap).

Year 3. S&P 500 Down: (20%). You make 0% (You don't lose in down years).

Year 4. S&P 500: 3%. You make 3%.

Year 5. S&P 500: 7%. You make 5% (100% growth up to the cap).

Some annuity companies will pay you a flat rate each year, if the index doesn't go down, which may be more advantageous to you in flat or stagnant years. Assume your flat rate is 4% and you have the following three years:

Year 1. S&P 500: 8%. You make 4%.

Year 2. S&P 500: 12%. You make 4%.

Year 3. S&P 500: 2%. You make 4%.

Some annuity companies also offer you the chance to have the index of your choice evaluated annually, or every two to three years. While you may be salivating at the thought of earning higher (than straight fixed) annuities, there are several things to consider before purchasing an indexed annuity.

You need to make sure you understand your length of contract and the withdrawal options, should you want or need to take funds out before the contract is up. Most annuities offer you some withdrawals or income without penalty. But the fees for taking too much out, or closing the account early, can be very high in an indexed annuity. As I just described above, you must make sure you understand how any possible returns will be calculated. If the annuity company offers you what's called a "point to point" strategy, they are looking at start to finish over a period of typically one to three years. No matter how many ups and downs you've seen in the market, what you earn will be based on the start versus the finish on your anniversary date. So, if the index were to take a huge decline a day, a week, or month before your anniversary date, you could see all your gains erased.

Variable Annuity

Variable annuities are, by far, one of the most misunderstood investments. I've often heard a variable annuity described as "an investment that some financial advisors understand, and no customer understands." I laugh each time I hear that because there's some truth to it. The variable annuity has several moving parts that are merged together, which often requires explanations and re-explanations. But I will give you a basic understanding of how the variable annuity works, and I'll abbreviate it going forward using "VA."

VAs take a combination of the opportunity of guarantees that a typical annuity offers, with the opportunity for growth of stock market investment choices. Whereas the indexed annuity provides your growth potential, but often limits your upside, the VA doesn't give you the "safety" of principal as the indexed annuity. But, in return, you have more upside growth. The interesting feature of VAs is that you can purchase various guarantees based on your family's needs. Often, the annuity company will also give you the opportunity to grow those guarantees over time until withdrawals are taken out of the contract. Similar to the indexed annuity, these guarantees are often referred to as riders, which can be a guaranteed amount of income, a guaranteed death benefit to your heirs, or protection from losses in the market. Once you begin to add these riders onto your contract, this is where the confusion often comes in.

When you receive statements, you may see multiple values on your statement. Before I give you an example, I want to explain how many of these riders function. Many of them will guarantee that your income value will increase by a predetermined percentage each year until you make a withdrawal, or within a number of years (i.e. 10 years). If, on your anniversary, the account value grows past the income rider, your income amount "steps up." Each year, your income value will be the higher of the account value, or a predetermined percent each year, until a withdrawal takes place. Many of the death benefits may function the same way.

Let's assume you make another $100,000 investment into a VA and purchase an income rider that guarantees your income value will increase by your highest anniversary value, or 5%, whichever is higher. Here's how that may look.

Contract Year	Investment Return	Account Value	Income Value	Death Benefit
Year 1	10%	$110,000	$110,000	$110,000
Year 2	3%	$113,300	$115,500	$113,300
Year 3	(10%)	$101,970	$121,275	$101,970
Year 4	(5%)	$96,871.50	$127,338.75	$100,000

As you view these past four years of your annuity, it's easy to see where you may get confused by looking at the statement. So, let's break down what each year would mean to you. For the sake of our conversation, assume you don't have an "enhanced" death benefit that's guaranteed to increase each year.

In the first year, we see your account going up 10%, which is more than the guarantee of 5%. So, now your account value and income value has increased to $110,000. You'll notice the death benefit is also at $110,000. That's because many of the VA contracts give a guaranteed death benefit, which will be the higher of your account value, or your original investment adjusted for withdrawals. In your case, no withdrawals took place.

In the second year, we still see a slight increase of 3%. But, since the income rider guarantees at least 5% per year in growth, your income rider goes up to $115,500, not the $113,300. Your death benefit is still $113,300 because it matches the account value, if it remains higher than your original investment.

In the third year, you unfortunately lost money. So, your account value is now $101,970. But your income value still grows by 5% to $121,275, and the death benefit will yet again match the account value because it's still higher than your original investment of $100,000.

In year four, you have another down year and your $100,000 investment is now worth $96,871.50. Your income value goes up yet another 5% to $127,338.75, but your death benefit goes back to $100,000 since your account is now worth less than what you originally invested. Let's assume your contract was only four years old, and now you're faced with multiple scenarios. Had you died at this four-year mark, your beneficiary would receive your $100,000 back, which is typical of variable annuities. If you were to receive income payments, the amount may be based on a withdrawal percentage of the income value. For consistency, let's say it's 5% of your income value of $127,338, or $6,367. If you decided you didn't want to receive the income, and you just wanted to walk away, you would receive the account value of $96,871.50.

The performance of your account is going to be a combination of investment options you choose. Many variable annuities give you a menu of options to choose from called sub-accounts, which are often based on the concept of mutual funds. You can usually build your portfolio, or pick one of the portfolios the company built, or do a combination of both. You'll find your traditional asset classes, such as stocks and bonds for both domestic and international companies, and many companies are now offering access to commodities like gold and silver. One thing to remember about VAs: Depending on your contract and any features you purchase, you may not have access to all the options the company offers. You may be limited on when and how you can change your portfolio after you set up the account. Some companies have measures in place that, if market volatility increases, the company can lower or limit your exposure to stocks and commodities, which are often the asset classes that have the most opportunity to grow.

As we look back at the features on variable annuities, and answer the million-dollar question, "How can they do this?", the answer is simple. They charge you. When annuities are purchased that income guarantees, they have historically ranged from 3-4% a year in fees. Newer ones have come to the market closer to 1-1.50%. These lower cost ones also have a unique feature that will often limit how much you can lose, while providing more upside than your typical fixed indexed annuities. These are called structured annuities. These structured annuities typically are offered at zero costs, until you add income or death benefit riders attached to them. They have become very popular over the years because investors have found they desire more upside than what their fixed indexed annuity provides, but also want some downside protection.

Stocks

Even if someone doesn't have any experience with personally investing in stocks, they still have some familiarity. When you turn on the news in the evening, you often hear quotes of the three major stock market indexes: Dow Jones Industrial Average, S&P 500 and NASDAQ. But after reading this section, my hope is that you have a better understanding of what you hear going forward. The stock market is a leading indicator of how well our economy is doing.

Stocks represent part ownership in a company. So, when you purchase shares of Microsoft, you actually own part of the company, along with your neighbors and the world-famous Bill Gates. Clearly, Bill Gates is the largest shareholder that is not a financial institution, and you and I are much smaller owners. Nonetheless, we're still owners. When you are an owner in a business, your number one goal is to see the company do well, grow and make money. As a stockholder of a company, the goal is the same, except you're not involved in day-to-day operations. As a shareholder, you still expect a return on your money. You have a vested interest in seeing the company do well, and the company's goal is to do well and see you satisfied as a shareholder. There are economic, international factors that will play a role in how well the company does. But, when you purchase stock in a company, you expect them to be able to navigate these waters and still return a profit.

Many times, an economy or industry may struggle. But there are always companies that manage to strive in any environment. So, whether you make or lose money will be directly tied to exactly how well a company is able to do. Stocks are the "Catch 22" investment. You could see your money grow immediately, or you could see it flop right away, especially if you're investing in a newer company. As you hold these shares of stock in the company, you will see the value of your shares go up and down based on how the company grows or contracts. Under normal market conditions, you can sell your shares at pretty much any time.

A simple tool to use is the finance section of yahoo.com. Use the pull quote box and type your favorite companies. Chances are, if their name does come up, they are publicly traded. If not, they may not publicly offer their shares. Two companies come to mind immediately that don't trade publicly: New York Life Insurance Company and Enterprise Rent-A-Car. This leads us to one of the simplest, yet profound pieces of advice you will receive about investing. Warren Buffett said, "Buy companies you're familiar with." As consumers, we're pretty brand-driven. We are loyal to certain companies. But, have you ever thought about being a part owner instead of a consumer to that company? How well has the company done over the past few years, and can you see them increasing in the near future? What's the consumer's opinion of the company and does the company have an edge on their competition? These are all basic, generic questions you want to consider as you approach buying stock.

When you invest in a company, you're essentially saying that you trust them with your money and overall livelihood. So, be sure to do your research. Stocks offer some of the best growth opportunities, but also carry substantial risk that could result in a loss of everything you put into the stock. Stocks fluctuate daily. You need to monitor your investments or pay someone to do it. Many publications will steer you away from individual stock picking; but regardless of what you invest in, it's important to work with professionally licensed advisors. Stocks trade in the open market. So, as you buy and sell them, you will have to pay commission, unless you have a different arrangement with your investment advisor. Remember those three things I said they talk about on the news? Let's reexamine them.

The Dow Jones Industrial Average is a stock market benchmark that is comprised of 30 of the most highly traded stocks. Again, when you have 30 of the largest publicly traded companies, you can get a feel for the overall direction of the stock market. Some of the 30 are Walmart, Apple and Disney. The S&P 500, like the Dow, is a benchmark. But it's comprised of 500 different companies. You may prefer to use a larger sample size. The NASDAQ, on the other hand, is made up of 100 different technology stocks. Some of the companies in the NASDAQ are also in the S&P 500 and Dow Jones. NASDAQ's largest holding as of 02/02/2018, are Apple, Microsoft, Amazon and Facebook. Remember, these are just benchmarks. There will be stocks that outpace and underperform them, but at least when you listen to the news, you'll be able to understand what it may mean to your portfolio.

At its most basic level, stock typically falls into two categories as it relates to style: growth and value companies. Growth stocks may be represented by either newer companies, or a company that has some leading technology that gives them a competitive edge. You may see rapid sales with the company, as well as quick upswings in the stock price. Growth stocks also typically invest heavy amounts of the company's earnings and/or investments into research and development to make the company stand out amongst its competitors. You may also see a particular company or group of companies quickly gain market share in their industry. Since the company is investing a significant amount into the development of the company, these "growth" stocks often do not pay dividends (partial return of profits). Many of the growth stocks come out of industries such as technology and pharmaceuticals. Some of the more common growth stocks are companies like Amazon, Google, Facebook, Netflix, and Tesla. The companies I named offer an opportunity to make your money grow, especially if you've invested early in the company. Growth stocks can also be market innovators and quickly grab large amounts of market share, as we've seen with companies like Google, Netflix and Facebook. As you can see, "growth" doesn't always mean the company is new. When you own growth companies, you may experience higher highs when things are going well, and lower lows when the economy as a whole is struggling. Growth companies can also be identified by companies who may grow higher than their competitors or the overall market.

In addition to growth stocks, you have "value" stocks. Value stocks get their name from the idea that investors may view them as undervalued based on defined criteria, such as the company's stock price, sales and earnings. Value stock buyers typically feel a particular company offers good, long-term potential, while their current stock price doesn't represent the true value of the company. Sometimes this is a company who may be profitable and experience growth, but the company stock price has gone down from bad press. If the company's financials suggest the company stock should be worth $15 per share, but it's $12, an investor may view this as a value stock. As we saw previously, growth stocks will typically reinvest much of their earnings back into the company. But value stocks will not only reinvest back into the company (retained earnings) but may return part of their earnings in the form of dividends back to their shareholders. How much you receive in a dividend will depend on the stock share price, how long you've held the stock, the amount of shares you hold and how much the company declares to pay as a dividend.

The dividend rate has a reverse relationship with stock price. As the stock price increases, the dividend rate will decrease. When the stock price falls, the dividend rate will increase. Typically, dividends are paid quarterly. As an investor, you can choose to reinvest the dividends back into the stock and buy more shares, or you can use it as another source of income. The dividend rate will vary across companies. But many times, you can have a more consistent income from value stocks than you will find in bank instruments. Of course, that comes with the risk of losing part, or all, of your investment. Many of your value stocks come from financial, food, utility and sometimes healthcare industries, to name a few. Historically though they may seem boring compared to growth stocks, value stocks have outperformed growth stocks.

The most common terms you'll hear as it relates to the size of a company are large, mid and small cap. At times, you may also hear the term mega cap. Market capitalization is a way to value a company by taking the stock price of a company and multiplying by the total shares outstanding of a publicly traded company. Suppose you have a company that has 10 million shares outstanding, and their share price is $35. This company has a market cap of $350 million. According to Investopedia.com, this company would fall into the category of a small cap company. Small-caps range from $300 million to $2 billion.

Mid-cap companies are $2 billion to $10 million and large-cap companies are those above $10 billion. Mega-caps don't have as much a straightforward definition, but examples would include companies like Apple, Google and IBM. While you may be familiar with many of the mega and large-cap companies, as you move to mid and small-cap companies, your familiarity with these companies will likely decline. Large-cap companies can be those who have long histories, like Coca-Cola, McDonald's or AT&T, while others can be those companies that have done well to differentiate themselves from their competitors. Mid-cap companies could either be those that have lost market share from a large-cap company, or companies that were previously small-cap companies.. Small caps, like mid-caps, are often companies who have seen growth and may offer opportunities to expand in the future. Some small caps may also be companies that have been on the market for a while, or companies that have recently allowed their shares to be offered in the public market.

However, you may also see more volatility in mid and small caps than some large caps.

There have been times, most notably in the early 2000s coming out of the dot com bubble, where the Russell 2000 small cap index showed less of a downside than the larger indexes like the Dow Jones Industrial Average and the S&P 500. Another identifier of the company you may invest in is a combination of both the type and size of the company. You may choose to buy a large-cap company like Google, or a small-cap dividend payer like Spartan Foods, which is a food distributor based in Michigan. As you can see, stocks literally come in different types, sizes and industries. While stocks do carry risk, they have historically not only outpaced the cost of living but have allowed many people to grow their wealth. Like everything else in life, it's a matter of knowing what you're doing or working with someone who knows what they're doing.

Mutual Funds

Even if people aren't familiar with how a mutual fund works, many have purchased them. This is the most common investment vehicle that is offered through company-sponsored plans, like 401(K), 403(B), 457 Plans, Thrift Savings Plans and small business plans like SEP & simple IRAs. Mutual funds are much older than most people think. There are some active funds from well-known companies such as Vanguard, Putnam and MFS that go back to the 1920s, or one of my favorites, Capital Group, that owns a company called American Funds.

Mutual funds are what I like to call the "dip your toe in the water" investment for those who either are new to investments, or those who don't want to deal with stock picking. At its most basic level, a mutual fund is a pool of money collected from a group of individuals. It is then turned over to an investment company to make the investment decision for those who invested into the fund. The mutual company will typically have fund managers who decide what investments will go into the fund. One thing to understand about mutual funds is that you don't directly own the investments within the fund. As an investor, you own shares of the fund and the mutual fund company owns the individual investments.

Assume that you bought "The Miller Mutual Fund" (I like the sound of that). It has a share price of $25. If you decided to put $10,000 into the fund, you would receive 400 shares of "The Miller Mutual Fund." Each mutual fund, whether it's new or seasoned, has a set objective, which you will often find in the fund's name. This will give you a good indication of what the mutual fund is purchasing. Depending on how active the fund manager is, there will often be times where they may sell one investment and purchase another. The mutual funds manager and company will decide where the company will invest, how much they will invest, and where they may refrain from investing. The age-old rule is to not put all your eggs in one basket. For many investors who aren't comfortable owning stocks or picking them, the mutual fund may be their ideal option because the fund can own anywhere from 50 different companies to 500. There's not a set amount that has to go in. However, many mutual funds require the company to not put more than 5% of all the funds collected into one company to manage the risk of the mutual fund.

Mutual funds can purchase everything from stocks, bonds, commodities like gold, or a combination of all the above. Some "specialty" funds may also buy things like stock options, futures contracts, currency or even other mutual funds. Since the mutual fund market has changed so much throughout the years, they can get as basic or as complex as you desire. Just like we described in our previous section on stocks, mutual funds will often fall into categories like size and type. This is an indication of what the mutual fund company's objection is and what it will likely purchase.

Mutual funds can also be described by the companies that are within the funds, such as companies in the U.S., those who hold only international companies based outside of the U.S., global companies, which will be a combination of both domestic and international companies, or funds that are specialized to certain territories like Asia, India and Africa. Mutual funds can also be very specific to industries like financial, healthcare, technology, food & beverage companies and more.

Mutual funds can also be categorized based on their management philosophy. Two common types you will find are passive and active management funds. Recall that each mutual fund has one or more managers who makes investment decisions for the fund's overall objective. However, there's still the question of how the company pursues that objective? That's where the management style and philosophy typically come into the equation. As the title suggests, passively managed funds may have changes in the fund periodically but, for the most part, the manager may not make constant changes within the fund. Some of the most common passive management funds are "indexed funds." Indexed funds are mutual funds that have the exact same holdings as a market index, such as the S&P 500. So, whatever the S&P 500 holds is what this same fund will hold. The only changes that will often take place is when a company changes within the index. An actively managed mutual fund is one where the fund manager/s will be more hands-on in their approach to managing the fund. You will see a lot more movement within the fund than what you would find in the passively managed fund. Though the fund's objective will stay the same, their approach to achieving it may change.

One year, the fund company may see growth opportunities in the pharmaceutical sector. The next year, they may shift more of their holdings into technology companies to pursue greater returns. Without getting too technical (though it may be too late), there may be within the investment strategy, strategic versus tactical management. Strategic management within a mutual fund may outline the fund to always have 50% in stocks and 50% in bonds. Although the actual stocks and bonds may change over time, the 50/50 allocation will typically stay the same. Tactical allocation will often set a range that says the fund can hold anywhere from 50-70% stock and 30-50% bonds. Based on current and future expected market conditions, the managers will make changes to take advantage of those changes. Whereas your portfolio at the start may be 50/50 between stocks and bonds, if they expect the stock market to continue to grow, they may change your allocation to 70% stock and 30% bonds.

Since we're dealing with an investment that has been around for almost 100 years, imagine how much things have changed over time. You may be asking yourself, "What mutual fund is right for me?" This is perfectly normal. Allow me to give you the pros and cons of a mutual fund. Then, you can decide if the option is right for you.

Pros

Diversification

Diversification is the first thing that comes to mind when you purchase a mutual fund. Even if the fund is specialized in a certain region or industry, the mutual fund will allow you to spread your money across different companies. Some mutual funds offer the opportunity to spread your money across companies of different types and sizes, as well as countries. These days, mutual funds have been designed to fit nearly every customer. You can purchase what's called an asset allocation fund that buys several types of investments based on the amount of risk you desire to take or when you need the funds. Some of these funds are called target funds because they build a portfolio and change the holdings as the target date approaches. Typically, the further away the target date is, the more aggressive the fund will be. Conversely, the closer the target date is, the more conservative the fund will likely be. Some of the most popular target funds will be in many 401(K) plans and 529 college plans because both usually have a designated or desired date where the funds are anticipated to be used.

Most people have a desired retirement age, as well as a set date they expect their children to enter college. Therefore, target funds are becoming more popular. A target fund is a cookie-cutter approach based on ages or dates. The target fund that correlates to your desired retirement age, or the year you expect your child to go to college, may be too aggressive for the risk you're willing to take. Also, the fund could be too conservative for you to achieve your financial goals.

Ease

Another positive aspect of mutual funds is the ease of investing on multiple levels. Since the investments that are purchased within the mutual fund are selected for you, you don't have to play the stock picking guessing game. Owning a mutual fund allows you to automatically contribute on a regular basis, without much thought and effort. It's very common to find investors who buy mutual funds on a monthly or pay-period basis, just like they send a specific amount of money to their savings account on a normal basis. Another neat aspect of automatic mutual fund purchasing is the fact that you can buy mutual funds in the specific dollar amount you want to invest in the fund. Many times, when you buy stocks, unless you're involved in employee stock purchase plans or automatic plans called "DRIP" plans, you may have to buy stocks in even share amounts. You may also be required to physically place orders each time you want to make a trade, which could be burdensome if you want to invest on a regular basis.

Access

Another staple of mutual funds is the access that they can provide to investors who are either just starting out, or those who want to begin investing in different areas of the market without taking on the full exposure themselves. Though the dollar amounts vary depending on the company you're considering, some companies allow you to start contributing for as little as $50. For those who may not be able to afford a large initial investment, this offers a great opportunity to get started. The small initial investment that may be available in mutual funds also goes hand-in-hand with access to different investments that you may not be able to buy on your own.

Suppose you wanted to invest in Warren Buffet's company, Berkshire Hathaway, but couldn't afford the $551,800 (as of 1/12/2023) price per share. You could buy a mutual fund that has its largest holding in Berkshire Hathaway. Even if you have the money, you may not want to invest that much money into one company. However, by purchasing a mutual fund, you can gain access to the shares. Due to regulation and diversification, the mutual fund may not own a large amount (i.e., more than 5%) in the one company you desire. Nonetheless, you'll still have some access to these different strategies. Lastly, access can come in the form of buying investments that you may have interest in, but are unsure how to purchase them, even if money wasn't a factor. You can purchase a mutual fund that trades foreign currency and decide that you want to dip your toe in the water, without making a large commitment to do so. I use currency as an example because it's one of those specialized areas where many people have questions. It could also be gold, silver, platinum, as well as alternative investment strategies. You may be surprised to see all that you can do with a mutual fund.

Liquidity

Another popular feature of a mutual fund is the typical quick turnaround to turn your money into cash, should you need to liquidate your funds. I will caution you to remember that mutual funds are long-term investments and shouldn't be used for short-term needs. However, liquidity is still a nice feature to have, especially when you consider that some of the funds may hold investments like real-estate that are not liquid investments, making them more difficult to turn into cash when needed. The type of mutual fund you own will determine where the liquidity primarily comes from, but the most common type of your everyday investment is an open-end mutual fund. When you purchase these mutual funds, you buy the shares directly from the mutual fund company. When you want to liquidate your shares, you're giving the shares back to the mutual fund company and the company, in turn, gives your cash back.

In closed-end mutual funds, the mutual fund company offers initial shares of the funds, similar to what you would find when a stock company first goes public. If you buy or sell shares after the initial offering, you're no longer dealing with the mutual fund company. You're buying and selling from different investors in the same manner when you trade stocks.

There are other benefits to buying mutual funds, but these are some of the most popular ones. Just as we discussed the good, we must also discuss some of the down sides. There's no perfect investment solution out there, and how "good" or "bad" something may be will be primarily based on your individual financial situation.

Cons

Although mutual funds offer diversification, that diversification does not necessarily mean your money is "safer." It doesn't prevent you from losing money when markets are down. The year 2008 was a big wake-up call for many advisors and investors. I know it's painful to even see those four digits right after each other. That year, major stock market indexes, like the S&P 500, were down nearly 40%. If you owned an indexed mutual fund, you were down just as much as the overall market. Even if you weren't in an index fund, if you owned a fund that primarily held stocks, you likely saw declines of anywhere from 20% to upwards of 40% or more. I say that because some of those specialty funds we discussed earlier were down more than the major market indexes. Even some of the asset allocation funds that hold various asset classes also experienced major drops. A mutual fund still carries risk. It's up to you and your advisor (if applicable) to understand the risks you may face by owning a particular fund.

Fees

The fees from mutual funds can be a pro or a con, depending on what funds you own. But because I've seen so many misunderstandings as it relates to the fee structures of mutual funds, I call them a con. Before we delve too deep into mutual fund fees, I want you to grasp the concept that these mutual fund/investment companies are not non-profit organizations. You would be surprised how many times I've asked clients what they are being charged for the funds they own, and they tell me, "I'm not being charged anything." I'm not making this statement to say the fee is a bad thing because the company must make money. But if you believe you aren't being charged anything, there's a good chance you're unaware of how you're being charged.

Mutual fund fees typically come in four different ways: front-load, no-load, back-end and internal. I will give a brief rundown of how each works. But keep in mind that no matter which fund you may own, they all have internal costs. Front-Loaded funds typically charge a fee upfront each time you purchase the fund. The amount will depend on how much you are investing, and how much you may already have invested in the company. No load funds are exactly as they sound, you don't pay upfront, but you may have a charge when you sell the fund. Back-end funds, which aren't as popular these days won't charge an upfront fee, but if you sell the fund within a certain timeframe, you may pay a fee. On top of these fees described, many mutual funds have internal costs called expense ratios. These are not always as clear, but are often present.

Lack of Control

The following statement can be very subjective because many people buy mutual funds to take the responsibility of buying and selling investments off their plate. But for those who want to be a bit more hands-on, the lack of control within a mutual fund can be viewed as a downside. When you own a mutual fund, the only thing you have control of is the fund you own, the amount you invest in the fund, and at what point you decide to sell the mutual fund. The mutual fund company decides what investments go into the fund. A mutual fund may purchase companies you disagree with, such as alcohol, tobacco or gambling companies. Mutual fund companies like Calvert and Dana Investment Advisors offer "socially and environmentally responsible" funds that may avoid investing in certain companies or industries. My point is you still can't control what they invest in. There could always be a company that you like which a mutual fund company may decide to liquidate. You also may not be able to find a mutual fund that holds the company you like. There may also be a situation where the mutual fund continues to hold stocks that you feel should be removed. Just like in our previous example, you must be comfortable with what the company decides.

Taxes

There may be other downsides relative to your financial situation, but my final point will be concerning taxes. I'm not an accountant and the intent of my following statements are not to be tax advice. You should seek the advice of a tax professional for your individual situation. In addition, the following information is only relative to *non-retirement* accounts that hold mutual funds. So, if you only own mutual funds in an IRA, 401(K), 403(B) or 457, this won't be as relevant. But the information is still vital because you may decide to purchase a mutual fund in a cash account. One of the down sides that can result from owning mutual funds in non-retirement accounts is the possible taxes that may be owed each year that you own the fund. Many times, when an investment is owned outside of a retirement account, you may have to pay capital gains taxes on your investment. Sometimes capital gains only occur when you sell your investment and it's sold at a profit. This is not the case many times for mutual fund owners, and it can become problematic, especially for high income earners.

In some cases, the company will replace companies and many times, these changes require liquidations within the fund. Even if you have not personally sold your shares of the mutual fund, you may find yourself receiving a tax bill. This becomes even more confusing in the years where the fund has declined, and you find your statement value going down. Yet, at tax time, you owe capital gains on your mutual funds that have lost value. Mutual funds can be simple or complex, and there are various components that need to be considered before and after purchasing them. My goal is not to sway you to buy them or avoid them, but to make you a more informed investor. That way you don't have to approach these decisions with fear, but with clarity and confidence. My hope is that you will be able to find a financial advisor who will walk you through these decisions, so you can understand all your options.

Exchange-Traded Funds

Exchange-traded funds (ETF) are a popular investment option that have been around for about 25 years. They've gained more popularity in recent years. ETFs, like many other investment options, come in different shapes and sizes. So, the information I provide will be very brief. I would encourage you to speak with a financial advisor to see if ETFs work for your financial goals.

ETFs work almost as a combination of both mutual funds and stocks combined into its own unique investment. ETFs often are created to mirror common market indexes like the S&P 500 and Russell 2000, and can also hold commodities like gold. ETFs have become more specialized over the years and provide access to many types of investments, but the idea is like a mutual fund. The investment company owns the basket of goods that the ETF gets its value from, but the ETF company allows purchases of units that correlate to the baskets of goods. Most ETF funds created have been passively managed because they either follow an index like the S&P 500, or they were based on a commodity like gold. Today, we see more actively traded funds.

In many cases, ETFs may be a lot cheaper to own, but that will vary by fund type. ETFs also trade throughout the day, like stocks. Typically, when a trade is placed during the market, you'll receive a valuation of your trade within a few seconds. Since the ETF is split up into different baskets based on the number of shares someone purchases, everyone essentially has a basket designated for them. This means ETFs may be more tax-efficient for investors in non-retirement accounts. There are several other technical aspects of ETFs that will be based on the fund. This isn't a recommendation to buy an ETF, but a push to speak with a financial advisor to determine if an ETF may work for you. Just like any other investment, there are risks. Most investments have market risk; however, there may be some risks associated specifically with ETFs that you need to review prior to any purchase. ETFs have become very popular because they offer the diversification of most mutual funds, but are often more liquid, less expensive, and more tax efficient than mutual funds. If you recall our previous view of mutual funds, you could owe capital gains taxes, even though you didn't sell your mutual fund. This would not typically happen in an ETF.

SECTION III
Inheritance Planning

12 Life Insurance Planning

There are several things you can do to make sure you engage in inheritance planning. The most basic comes in the form of life insurance. Recent studies show that, on average, many people either don't have life insurance or they don't have enough. This should be alarming. Many of us have heard something about life insurance. Some people have owned a life insurance policy at some point. Life insurance is one of those tricky things because, depending on what type of policy you have, and the age and health you have at the time you take the policy out, it could be one of the lowest expenses you have. Yet, many people don't have life insurance. Even as I describe this as an expense, I want you to view it as an investment in your family's inheritance. I know there's some creepy apprehension about discussing life insurance, but I assure you that the conversation and purchase doesn't shorten your life, nor does *not* buying life insurance extend your life. The dangerous part of not having life insurance is the fact that when you have a need for life insurance, delaying it only gets more expensive, which could in turn convince you to not buy it. I'm not a gambling person, but even if I were, that's not a bet I would be willing to make because my family's well-being is riding on it.

Purchasing life insurance isn't complicated if you're working with the right advisor. Making sure you have the correct coverage and policy is a bit more involved than what one may think.

The first step is to sit down and talk with either a financial advisor or an insurance agent. I typically would consider an advisor or agent who is "independent" and can offer you life insurance from multiple companies, not just the one they work for. Sometimes when you're working with an agent who works for a company that offers their own life insurance policies, there may be a natural inclination to steer customers to that company's products. Also, if the company can only offer you their product, you have no way of knowing if that company is the best fit for you. Their prices may not be as competitive as other companies. Don't make your decision solely on price, but don't ignore price either. When you work with an independent agent, they often have the ability to shop rates to see who will give you the type of coverage you need for the best price available.

Another benefit of working with an independent company is that the agent can also share experience when dealing with other insurance companies that may affect your decision to buy life insurance through them. Buying life insurance isn't just about price; there are other things to consider when you purchase a policy.

You will want to consider how long the company has been in business. Review their customer satisfaction ratings and explore how long they take to pay claims. Research the company's credit rating from agencies such as Standard & Poor's, Moody or Fitch. Also, review the company's balance sheets. Obviously, this is a lot of information to consider, but the bulk of the responsibility is on your insurance agent. However, these are questions you should ask. To make things basic, I would suggest that purchasing life insurance is a three-step process. First, you must determine the amount of life insurance you need. Secondly, determine how long you need the life insurance. Finally, determine the most economical way to accomplish steps one and two.

I want to stress to you the importance of working with seasoned professionals who will take the time to advise you. While I respect my clients' opinions and feelings, I refuse to sell someone a life insurance policy simply because they walk in my office and say, "Here's what I want."

I commonly find that when people purchase life insurance, they tend to want to keep the costs on the low side. Some people have numbers associated with either the amount of coverage they want or the amount of money they should pay monthly, without putting much thought into it. Don't work with someone who is simply taking your order. If someone is willing to sell you what you want above what you need, that person is not looking out for your family's best interest. I would personally let a potential client walk out the door before I would knowingly give them incorrect financial advice. Calculating how much life insurance you need is often done using financial software. However, there is other information you will need to provide to your agent as they help you plan. An easy to use, yet effective tool is a website called lifehappens.org. If you go to this website and click on calculators, you will find the life insurance needs calculator.

How Much Life Insurance Do You Need?

To answer this question, you must think about where you are financially today, where you want to be in the future, and the financial ramifications of you not being here. First, consider what you want the life insurance policy to accomplish for you and your family. Consider not only the aspect of paying for funeral expenses, but also take into consideration paying off your home, car notes and student loan debt. Do you want to replace your income for several years, cover living expenses for your family for so many years, pay for your children's education, or all of the above?

Let's assume we have a couple, Mike and Samantha, who are both 40. They have two children, Mike Jr., who is four years old, and Zoey, who is two. Mike makes $60,000 as an electrician, and Samantha is a stay-at-home mom. They have a mortgage on their home of $150,000, a $15,000 car loan and

$35,000 in combined student loan debt. Luckily, they don't have any credit-card debt. Nonetheless, both Mike and Samantha want to make sure the family is taken care of if they were to die unexpectedly. To keep the math simple, let's assume they have no other life insurance or savings. Mike desires to make sure that his family's debts are paid off, and he doesn't want Samantha to have to go back to work to take care of the children. He would prefer for her to continue to stay at home with the children until they're through their college years. Mike also wants to make sure his life insurance policy would set aside money for the children's higher education and a retirement account for Samantha. Mike considers that if he were to pay off all his family's debt, it would cost the house $1,500 a month, but he also wants to set aside $1,041 per month to put away for Samantha's retirement. So, let's see how Mike determines how much life insurance he should buy.

Debt: Household Expenses

Using the lifehappens.org calculator, Mike's need for life insurance is about $1,083,000.

The breakdown looks like this:

Funeral = $10,000

Debts = $50,000

Mortgage = $150,000

College Funding = $315,424.15

Total Lump sum = $ 525,424.15

Income Needs = $30,500 ($1,500 monthly expenses plus Samantha's $1,041 monthly retirement savings)

This income is needed for 20 years, and we also assume the cost of living increased by 3% per year.

We also assume we can get a return of 4% per year on the proceeds from the life insurance

The present value of the future income needs = $ 557,366.11

If we combine our lump sum need of $525,424.15+ our income need of $ 557,366.11, we arrive at the number of Mike's life insurance need of $ 1,082,790.26

If the tables were turned and Samantha passed, Samantha's goal is to still pay for the children's education, pay off debt and pay for private school for both children until they get to college. Samantha estimates the cost for private school will be $16,000 per year for Mike Jr. and Zoey, or $1,334 per month. Mike will still be able to work and save for his own retirement because, with no debt, the family household budget would only be $1,500 per month, but to be safe Samantha wants this to be available for 20 years and assume Mike has nothing saved for retirement

The lump sum number for Samantha will be the same as Mikes because her goal of paying off debt and savings for the kids' education is unchanged.

Where the numbers differ is on the income need.

Samantha desires for $34,000 ($18,000 living expenses plus $16,000 for private school)

Samantha desires this $34,000 for 20 years, while also assuming the annual increase in the cost of living is 3%, while still earning 4% on the life insurance proceeds.

The present value of the future income need calculates at $621,326.15 + the lump sum need of $ 525,424.15 gives us a total life insurance need of

$ 1,146,750.30. What's different is we must factor in the present value of Mike's income over the years = $ 822,343.43

We take our total life insurance need of $ 1,146,750.30 and subtract Mike's income of $ 822,343.43 and we can determine the life insurance need for Samantha at $ 324,406.87

Are those numbers alarming to you? Although this is a technical version of what should really happen, it shows you that calculating how much life insurance you need is not as clear cut as it may seem. In real life, you must consider some of the same things as Mike and Samantha. But you also want to make sure you consider your income, current assets, monthly expenses and much more. While there are other things to consider when calculating the amount of life insurance you'll need, one caveat I would suggest is excluding part, if not all, retirement assets from the equation. Accessing retirement funds to pay off debt and to live may not be very favorable because of the taxes on those accounts. Nonetheless, work with professionals who will walk you through this step and the entire process. There are several other simple calculations like 20 times your salary. If you make $50,000 a year in income, a baseline could be $1,000,000 in life insurance.

How Long Do I Need Life Insurance?

This is the million-dollar question. The quick answer is, "It depends." Answering this question will also lead you toward a hunch on what type of life insurance you may need (which we will discuss later). Answering this question is solely based on your individual needs. This should not be approached using a cookie-cutter approach or general formula. Consider if you have a mortgage on your home that will be paid off in 25 years. If your goal is to make sure the house will be paid for if you die. A 25-year policy may be the right fit. In Mike and Sam's situation, where Mike wanted to make sure he could cover his children's education costs. Maybe insurance for 15 or 20 years would work.

However, what if you are in a situation where it is difficult for you to calculate when the need would go away? What if you're in a scenario where the need would not go away at all, like Mike needing to save for Samantha's retirement? What if you are caring for a special needs relative? Clearly, in the special needs case, that need won't go away. So, buying a policy for a specific amount of time may not work.

Determine the Most Cost-Efficient Way to Achieve Your Goal

When we get to this step, most people have two choices: buy term life insurance or permanent life insurance. As we approach this topic, I would caution you on entering this with any biases you may have because both fit a need. The general rule of thumb is typically to buy term insurance for temporary needs, and permanent life insurance for permanent needs.

Term Insurance

Term life insurance is exactly how it sounds, for a specific predetermined time. If we go back to our example of paying off a home in 25 years, one could simply buy a term life insurance policy for 25 years to match up with the time horizon. Once the 25 years are up, you may not have any more life insurance. It's like renting life insurance, which doesn't necessarily make it bad. If your only concern was to pay off the mortgage and nothing else, once those 25 years have passed, you may not want life insurance anymore. Term insurance can range from 30 days to 30 years, and it's typically the least expensive form of life insurance you can buy. This is because the insurance company can calculate the risk of taking you on as a customer because the period is defined. With term life insurance, most companies allow you the option to convert some or all of your policy to permanent insurance at predetermined dates, without having to go through another medical exam. Others allow you to renew once your term is up, but the premium at that point is likely unaffordable. There are various types of term policies where your premium can stay the same throughout the term or gradually increase every few years.

With term life insurance, the most important thing to remember is that once your term is up, unless you extend your policy or convert to a different type, you may no longer have any life insurance coverage. Remember, the main thing is to buy term for temporary needs. But you also must consider term for affordability issues. From personal experience, if ten people come in for a review, nine of them are underinsured. As we saw in Mike and Samantha's case, it's quite easy for a couple or individual who has dependent or minor children to need over a million dollars in coverage. The same is true for some business owners. You find people on both sides. Some love term and hate permanent insurance, and vice versa. But before you discard term, it may be the only thing you can do to ensure you're fully insured. For those who love permanent insurance, they hate the fact that after the term policy is up, they no longer have insurance. They would much rather buy a permanent policy to know for certain that they always have coverage. My motto is, "It's better to be temporarily fully insured than to be permanently underinsured."

Whole Life Insurance

Term insurance seems to be the type most people are familiar with, but there are different types of permanent life insurance. The most common is whole life. This life insurance policy pays a stated amount at the insured's death, and it can be purchased with either a lump sum of money or periodic payments. Though some joke and call it whole life because they say, "You'll be paying on it for your whole life," there are various ways to purchase a whole life policy. You can purchase it in a lump sum, pay for it over the span of your life, or you can buy what are called paid up policies where your payments are accelerated. You pay your policy off over a span of 10, 20, 25 years.

There are a couple of things to consider with a whole life policy. One of them is the fact that you will pay more upfront because the life insurance company must insure you for your entire life (if you continue to pay). Although they have people who calculate probabilities, they don't know whether you'll live another 100 years or 100 days. So, they must price the policy to properly assume that risk. What makes whole life different from term is the fact that whole life has a cash value component to the policy.

There are several ways life insurance policy premiums are calculated. But, to keep it basic, we'll focus on the cost of insurance. The cost of insurance is exactly as it sounds, the cost to cover your life. Within a term policy, that's most of your premium. However, within whole life, it's just a part of it and the cash value is the other part. In your early years, you may not see much growth, if any, in the cash value portion of the policy (depending on the company and type of whole life you own) because more of the premium goes towards the cost of insurance. Typically, after several years have passed, you'll see the cash value build up. The cash value typically earns interest and will continue to build throughout the life of the policy. As you hold the policy longer, you'll see more increase in the cash value balance.

Let's assume Mike decided he wanted a $250,000 whole life policy. He paid on this policy for 20 years and, for the purpose of conversation, we will ignore any possible policy dividends or increases in the death benefit. By then, Mike's policy still has a death benefit of $250,000, but his cash value is $75,000. Mike can borrow that $75,000 and do whatever he wants with it. But if he never pays it back, and then dies, the life insurance company would deduct that $75K + interest, then pay Samantha. If the interest was $5,000, Samantha would get $170,000, which is the $250,000 minus $75,000 minus $5,000 interest. I know by now you're probably thinking, "What happens to that $75,000 if Mike never takes the money out and he dies?" Remember, the risk has shifted on Mike's end. Whereas if Mike died in the early years of the policy, the insurance company would be basically paying the death benefit out of their own money.

In the latter, where Mike has built up the cash value, the insurance company would pay the $250,000 to Samantha by adding $175,000 of their own money, as well as taking Mike's cash value and adding to the $175,000.

Under normal circumstances, most whole life policies pay dividends, which are just a partial return of the insurance company's profits. Those dividends can be used to buy more insurance, buy a term policy, or just pay the dividends to you in cash. I want to reiterate that many have an issue with the cash value not being paid at death, but in a dividend paying policy, that cash value has likely grown to the point where it has also increased the value of the policy to increase.

Again, this is a very simplistic approach to this subject. However, note a few things. You must remember that if you do have cash value, cash value is a living benefit. So once the policy owner dies, the insurance company will not pay both the death benefit and the cash value. Only the death benefit.

There are a couple of additional things to consider with owning whole life insurance policies:

1. Though it's often determined by your budget, you're choosing what you want to purchase. So, you're in control.
2. Because you're often withdrawing contributions, dividends from the policy, or taking loans against the death benefit, the use of cash value is often a non-taxable event when structured properly. This often makes for a very effective way to save for retirement, educational planning, business planning or just flexibility in future years, in addition to the legacy planning aspect of buying life insurance.

The cash value portion of the life insurance contract always has a guaranteed amount, which means you know it will grow, even if it's by a modest amount. I know you may be thinking "What do people use this cash value for." The quick answer is it depends, but the cool thing is it can be used for whatever reason you desire. Here are 4 common places where cash value is utilized.

Emergency/Loan

Sometimes people need quick access to cash without liquidating investments or triggering taxes, so for flexibility, some use their cash value. When withdrawn correctly as described above, you can access a portion of what's available and pay it back if you choose. Sometimes if you take a loan on your policy you may find the interest rate is lower than what it would be on traditional loans.

Education

Again, when money is withdrawn correctly from cash value life insurance, not only can you avoid paying income taxes on the transaction, but as it sits now, it wouldn't negatively impact financial aid if you have a student because it's not considered an asset for your family's expected contribution.

Retirement Supplement

What happens when you go into retirement and you're drawing assets from an account that's declining in value? Not knowing this answer, or not having a strategy around this scenario could threaten the longevity of your assets and the comfort of your retirement. If you have another source of money that you can access in down markets, you may be able to allow your other assets to recover and increase their longevity.

Business Planning

I'll touch on this briefly in the life insurance for business owners section, but permanent insurance is also used in business planning where a partnership agreement states if one partner dies the other partner takes over. This is common, but how do you provide capital if one of the business owners divorces, wants to retire, or does something illegal? The temptation may be to say the business assets will buy out the other partner, but what if the business can't afford this financial strain. There are many other scenarios that business owners must consider, but succession plans are a very common place to find permanent insurance.

Universal Life

Another type of permanent life insurance that can be a bridge between both term life and whole life is universal life. Universal life insurance sometimes offers flexibility that you may not find in whole life. But, universal life insurance may provide you with the lifetime coverage you desire. Though universal life does offer a cash value component, you may not see it grow as fast as whole life. More money goes toward the cost of insurance, which keeps your premiums lower than whole life. The flexibility offered in universal life insurance policies often comes in the form of the company allowing you to adjust your death benefit permanently, or your premium for a period of time without necessarily lowering the death benefit. The insurance company will typically tell you the minimum amount you need to pay to make sure the policy doesn't end, but you could also pay more in the policy for either extra flexibility in the future, or to build up a larger cash value.

Just like term life insurance, you must make sure you understand your policy. Your premiums may increase over time, which may cause your policy to become unaffordable. Even though they're advertised as permanent life insurance, some universal life policies will only cover you to certain ages (i.e., 85, 90, 100.) Also, if you don't make the minimum payments, or the assumed rate of interest isn't earned, your policy could lapse, or the premium could increase. So, if you're considering a UL policy, you likely want to seek out a level UL. You will still have the option of making changes in the future.

There are other permanent policies, like variable life and variable universal life that add investment components like mutual funds in the mix. I won't get into details, but I encourage you to speak with a licensed agent who also holds a securities license if it piques your interest. If you're looking for permanent insurance and are mostly concerned with the cheapest premium and not cash value, a universal life policy may be the way to go.

Buy Term and Invest The difference

Before we go any further, let's take a pause and address the elephant in the room. Throughout this book my goal is to be both fair and balanced with each subject manner by giving both the good and the bad to the various options in financial planning. I'll approach life insurance the same way, but I want to unpack the phrase "buy term and invest the difference." Some ask for my professional opinion, while others are presenting a loaded question to try and bait me into a debate. If this is new to you, allow me to explain. Buy term and invest the difference is the idea that instead of buying permanent insurance, buy term, and the difference that you would pay in permanent insurance should be invested. To take it a step further, the thought is instead of depending on the growth of the cash value in a permanent policy, the investment you could potentially invest in would grow at a faster rate, eliminating the need for the permanent coverage in the future. Let's break this down numerically so it makes more sense.

Assume, you have a 40-year-old woman with a standard health rating who has a need for life insurance of $500,000. She's presented with two options, term life and whole life. The term life would provide her coverage for 30 years and would cost her about $100 per month. Her other option is whole life which would provide her lifetime coverage and would cost $600 per month. We can see the difference in cost is about $500 per month. Though the whole life policy provides lifetime coverage and builds cash value that the owner can use. The proponents of "buy term and invest the difference" would argue this person probably doesn't need lifetime coverage and would be better off having the $500,000 in coverage temporarily, while having this investment vehicle on the side that's accumulating along the way. Some also have somewhat of a cynical view of agents and believe the only reason they are being offered permanent life insurance is so the agent can earn a higher commission. On the surface, "buy term and invest the difference" may be a logical conclusion, but when dealing with financial planning one must go beyond the surface. Let's review four angles that must be considered to determine if buy term and invest the difference will work for you.

1. **Is your goal with life insurance temporary or permanent?**

Many times, people set inheritance goals where they are sure no matter what, they want to leave an inheritance to their kids, community, or church. Within the context of buy term and invest the difference, the assumption is those assets will grow that you can leave behind, but what if the assets you accumulate are needed for other things like your retirement? What if you have a special needs child that needs to have assets set aside permanently?

2. **Are you disciplined enough to consistently save the difference each month over a long period of time?**

a. This is the biggest problem with "buy term and invest the difference," Are you really going to invest the difference? Remember, this is not money going into a 401K, but rather is being invested outside of those accounts to take the place of what would otherwise be accumulating in a permanent life insurance policy. I've seen many who may have started investing the difference. Then something happens in life and they never start back up. These people get towards retirement and realize they now have life insurance that will end, and many times they haven't accumulated the assets they expected. They still have a need for the insurance, but they now may be either uninsurable because of changes in health. Or, age alone may have increased the premium to the point they believe it's unaffordable.

b. Aside from potential lifetime coverage, the permanent policy is a forced savings which means if you don't pay the premium you don't have your coverage. If we're honest enough to recognize we're not financially disciplined, this may be what you need. Remember, you can stop investing the difference at any point without noticing the impact until later.

3. **How will you guarantee an inheritance?**

Remember Proverbs 13:22 admonishes us to leave an inheritance to our children's children, so how do we make sure that happens? With technology and an aging population, you may need all the assets you accumulate over time to care for your needs. This question also connects to the previous two. If we look back to our scenario of the 40-year-old woman who decides to buy the term and invest the difference. For her to accumulate the same $500,000 in assets she would have to diligently save roughly $500 per month for 30 years and earn on average 6% per year on that money. Not only do you have to save the money, but you also must be comfortable taking risk with the money to try and earn at least the 6% to grow the assets. Keep in mind you're likely paying taxes on this money along the way, which eats into the interest you earn each year. Also keep in mind the permanent policy, may have not only accumulated a cash value you can use for anything you want, but the death benefit may have grown as well.

Does buying term and invest the difference make sense and work? Maybe, but whether it makes sense depends on variables specific to your life. This is yet another situation that needs to be discussed with a professional who is licensed, experienced, and understands your goals. The idea that everyone should do the same thing is dangerous. The thought that no one needs permanent insurance is simply bad advice. Lastly, just because someone will earn compensation on the transaction doesn't mean buying permanent insurance is not right for you. Keep in mind the same advisor who's telling you to buy term and invest the difference is earning compensation on both the term and the investment options.

As we've already discussed, to make your life insurance purchase most impactful, make sure you're working with a professional (you can verify this through your state's insurance department). Preferably, work with one who is independent of any one company. Work with an agent who can offer both term and permanent insurance because everyone's situation is unique. Unfortunately, some agents can be biased. They believe that people should only have term or only have permanent insurance, and your situation may call for both. So, make sure whomever you work with walks you through the process as described above. Another aspect of purchasing life insurance is to do your research on, not only your agent, but the company they work for and the life insurance company they're proposing to you.

Bigger is not always better, but you do want to be careful with your decision. It does you no good to get all the way up to this point and select a life insurance company that goes out of business because they didn't properly manage their affairs. So, the size of the company is a valid consideration. You may also want to consider how long the company has been in business. Many of the well-known life insurance companies have been around since before the stock market exchange was established. They have survived The Great Depression, multiple stock market crashes, multiple world wars and countless presidents.

Another consideration is how other customers view this insurance company. As with most sales, people are typically kind, responsive and professional when they're trying to close a deal. But you want to see how people are treated after the fact. Does the company respond in a timely manner? Do customers find them kind and attentive, and how easy is it to collect proceeds in death situations? Again, these are things your agent should be discussing with you. If they aren't, you might want to consider either researching these items yourself or reviewing your policies with another agent.

Life Insurance for Small Business Owners

Throughout this book, you'll see me make special notes for small business owners because I know that planning will be different for business owners. I want to make sure I don't neglect your needs in my attempt to make this book relevant for all readers. As a business owner, your life insurance process is going to follow the same steps as a non-business owner; however, it will entail more work because you must segment your policies for the business, as well as your personal life insurance policies. As a business owner, I know life and business can sometimes seem to merge. But there are both personal and business aspects of life, and they must be treated financially the same way. Just like we did in the previous examples, you want to make sure you take the same steps of figuring out how much life insurance you need, how long you need it, and what the most efficient, economical way to accomplish the job is. As a business owner, you must think through the same situations as it relates to the business.

For one, you must think about what your desires for your business would be if something were to happen to you. Would you want the business to be sold, to be given to a partner, or to be kept in your family? You also must consider how much your business is worth and what type of financial shape the business is in. It's important that you have some type of business valuation completed to answer these questions. Otherwise, the information I'm going to follow will be limited by its impact on your bottom line.

Let's assume you own a business with a partner, 50/50. You both are married and personally respect each other's spouse. But, should one of you die, you have no desire to run a business with your partner's spouse. This business is worth $5,000,000. Each partner decides to own a 2.5-million-dollar life insurance policy on the life of the other owner. If your partner dies, the policy would be used to essentially buy your partner's shares of the business out and pay the proceeds to his family. You now completely own the business and his family is taken care of. Everyone is happy, and everything was completed as you two desired. This is, in part, estate planning. But remember how you were able to set this up: through life insurance planning. What you just read is what is affectionately known as business succession planning through buy/sell agreements.

The agreement was for your partner's estate to sell all of his shares to the business upon his death. The business is purchasing the shares and the life insurance policy is used to come up with the cash to buy the family out. One of the many things to remember when operating under buy/sell agreements is that they need to be periodically reviewed and updated. Whether up or down, good or bad, very few, if any, businesses stay the same in value. So, it's important that you have your business re-evaluated every 3-5 years at the latest. This not only ensures proper valuation of the business, but also makes sure the agreements are properly funded through the correct amount of life insurance.

Another piece that is very close to a buy/sell agreement is Key Person Insurance. Key person, or key man, insurance is used to compensate a business for losses that are a result of the death or disability of a key person. There's no straight definition of who the "key-person" is. If it's your business, you must determine who that person is. Who is irreplaceable to your business? Does your business have a proprietary process or product that only one person out of few people truly understand in your organization? Is there anyone who is so important to your day-to-day operations that the business would be in big trouble should you lose that person? As the business owner, is it you? If you look around, it's easy to spot the key person. Make sure you have coverage, just in case something unexpected happens to that person.

13 Educational Planning

Educational planning can seem difficult at times because just the thought of paying for school for a loved one can be overwhelming. I have five children under the age of 11 years old, so I know the feeling. While there are always unique and creative ways to save for school, I will primarily focus on options that are designated specifically for school.

Educational Savings Account/Coverdell

The educational savings account (ESA) or Coverdell account allows you to save for educational expenses, while allowing you to choose investment options. An ESA can either be a bank account or an investment account. Your options will depend on what the bank or investment custodian you utilize can hold.. You could open an ESA as a savings account or buy individual stock or mutual funds. ESA funds can be used for elementary, secondary schools, or higher post-secondary education, like college. Currently (2018) the most you can contribute is $2,000 per child per year, and that child must be under the age of 18. Contributions must be made by the time you file your taxes, and like retirement accounts, there are contribution income restrictions along with the contribution limits. If your income is above these thresholds, you may find that your contributions would be reduced. In addition, you may be restricted from making any contributions.

Typically, funds that are held in ESA accounts grow tax-deferred and qualified educational expenses are withdrawn income tax free, as long as the distribution doesn't exceed your actual educational costs. Allowable expenses depend on whether it's higher education or elementary and secondary schools.

Under higher education, your common qualified costs are things like tuition, room and board, books, special needs services, supplies, and possibly computer equipment, technology and software. Elementary and secondary qualified expenses are very similar, except you would take out the room and board and add things like tutoring, uniforms and transportation. The list will vary based on your situation. So, make sure you speak with an accountant and financial advisor to ensure you coordinate an ideal situation for yourself.

When funds leave an ESA that aren't qualified, you may be subject to taxes and a 10% penalty that you see on early withdrawals from retirement accounts. However, there are still ways to possibly avoid this tax and fees ahead of time. As we discussed, the child you're opening the account for must be under 18, but the funds don't have to be fully withdrawn until 30 days within their 30th birthday. In a situation where the child won't need the funds, you also have the option of transferring the funds to another relative under the age of 30. The person doesn't have to necessarily be an immediate family member. If you invested in your ESA account, and lost money after the account is empty, you may be able to deduct those losses on your taxes.

ESA/Coverdell accounts are a popular option for people who aren't sure which path their loved one will take. They still have flexibility to use the funds for non-college educational expenses. After reviewing your situation, you may find that an ESA is an option for you on its own or alongside some of the options that are for higher education expenses.

529 Plans

529 plans receive their title from IRS codes that identify that they are for higher education. While there are some similarities with 529 plans, there are basically two types of 529 plans available: prepaid tuition plans and investment/savings plans.

Prepaid Tuition Plan

Whereas many of the investment and savings plans allow you a lot of flexibility to decide your contributions, you decide ahead of time how much of your loved one's tuition you want to pay for today. Since the cost of education has consistently gone up each year, the prepaid tuition plans allow you to lock in today's tuition rates, though your loved one may not be headed to school for quite a few years. There are various levels of plans you can buy that would cover the basic costs of community college, up to more expensive packages that would cover all state schools. They may cover all, or a good portion of, private in-state schools, as well. Once you determine what package you want to purchase, decide how many semesters you want to pay for. Some of the plans allow you to purchase up to five years' worth of semesters. Once you've decided on the package and the number of semesters, choose your payment option. Many times, you can pay in a lump sum or pay over a number of years, like a mortgage payment. The payment schedule could be as short as a few years or longer term, like 15 years. It costs you more if you're paying the balance over a period of time versus if you were paying it in a lump sum. However, that periodic payment may be the only choice.

The cost of education is expensive, so you have to start with a payment you can afford. Review if that payment falls into one of the plans available. Let's take my situation, for example. In the state of Michigan, if I were to pre-pay for four years of college for my children at their current ages, the cost today (2018) would be roughly $70,000 per child. If I elected to pay it over 10 years, the total amount would be $816 per month, for a total of $97,920. Over 15 years, it would be $640 per month for a total of $115,200 per child.

There are no perfect solutions, but there are options. There are other features that are typical of a prepaid tuition plan. As the title describes, these plans typically will only cover tuition and necessary fees associated with tuition. So, you will likely still have to save or borrow for things like room and board for your student. Needs and ideas change, so there isn't pressure to use the funds right away. Your student has 10 plus years after high-school graduation to use the funds. Another common feature is the ability to transfer the funds to an immediate family member should your student not need the funds. Who counts as an immediate family member may vary from state to state. A common guide is a parent, sibling and, in some cases, cousins.

If you find no one uses the funds, refunds are available. Keep in mind that when you contribute to a state-sponsored plan, you'll usually receive some sort of deduction on your state income taxes. When you use the state-sponsored plan, your student often has to choose a school within the same state. If, for some reason, they decide to go to a school outside your state of residency, all is not lost. However, you may not receive the full benefits. Not all states offer a prepaid 529 plan. There are other prepaid tuition plans available, so make sure you speak with a financial advisor to learn about other options.

529 Investment/Savings Plans

The 529 investment/savings plan works differently than a prepaid tuition plan. It is very much similar to a retirement account, except it is used for higher education. There are many state-sponsored plans available, but you aren't required to use your state plan (if applicable). In the state-sponsored plan, (if you decide to use your plan) there will be some tax benefits available each year you contribute to the plan. Another similarity between these plans across states is tax-deferred growth while the money sits in the account. As long as the money is used for educational expenses, your withdrawals are tax-free. Those expenses can range from tuition, lab fees, and room and board. If you withdraw money that isn't considered a qualified withdrawal, you may be subject to taxes, plus a 10% penalty on any gains withdrawn. Since you don't have federal tax deductions on your contributions, your original investment into the account has already been taxed.

Suppose that I've invested $10,000 into a 529 plan. Over the years, it grew to $20,000 and I withdrew the money to buy a car for my daughter. Since this isn't a qualified tuition expense, I would have to pay taxes and a 10% penalty on my $10,000 worth of gains.

Another difference in the 529 savings plans is the flexibility in the amount you invest. Many of the plans allow you to contribute as little as $25 upfront, if you continue to contribute $25 per month. It also allows you to make lump sum payments along the way if you choose to, assuming you don't contribute more than what gift tax laws allow. Most plans also allow you to make a 5-year contribution at once, which would allow a dump in of approximately $75,000. There's a lot more flexibility with your contributions in this plan. You may be asking yourself, "Where is the money going?" Within this question lies probably the biggest distinction between the prepaid tuition plans and the savings plans.

In the prepaid tuition plan, you know ahead of time what benefit you're going to receive based on the amount of your contribution and time frame. Within the savings plans, you're investing the money into mutual-fund like accounts, just like you would find in your IRA/401(K) plans. This means you don't have a guaranteed outcome. The value of your investment will fluctuate up and down, but there are typically multiple options available in the plan, from conservative to aggressive options. Some of the plans do have a "guaranteed rate option," which doesn't fluctuate. This will pay a fixed rate of interest, but that interest rate will change. You can always choose to build your own portfolio or use one of their pre-built portfolios. The portfolios are often diversified based on risk tolerance, where the most conservative options have less stock and more fixed income options, like bonds. The aggressive options have more stocks, international and alternative investments.

Another common option is "age-based" portfolios, where the investments will automatically change the closer your loved one gets to the time they will go to college. For example, an age-based portfolio for a five-year-old will be more invested into stock funds because the first withdrawal wouldn't take place for at least 13 years (age18). The portfolio for a 15-year-old will be more conservative because the time frame is much shorter, and you don't have as much time to make up losses. Another consideration with the 529 savings plans are the associated fees with the plan. Since these are investments, there may be annual fees from the plan. Whatever fund you elect, there will be an internal operating cost (expense ratio) on the fund. If you're working with an advisor, there may be an upfront or deferred fee, as described in the mutual fund section.

As we described in the prepaid tuition section, you have several years after high school to use the funds for school. You also have the option to transfer the funds to a relative in case the person you originally set the plan up for doesn't need the funds. One distinction between the 529 savings plan and the prepaid tuition plan is that even if you don't use your state-sponsored 529 savings plan, the funds can still be used at any college. You just lose out on possible state tax deductions (if applicable). There are a bunch of savings plans to choose from. You would have to sit down and consider what you can afford, your time frame, how much flexibility you have and need, as well as the possible fees associated with the plan. You may find that it's worth using an out-of-state plan if the fees are lower and the returns are higher. When the Trump administration changed the tax laws, 529 plans became available for use before your student becomes a college student. For example, if you wanted to send your children to a private high school, you can now use funds in a 529 plan to cover the expense, which is another incentive to use 529 plans to save for your children's education.

Many people use 529 plans as estate planning tools. Many wealthy families, who have a large amount of assets or owe taxes each year, use contributions to 529 plans for their loved ones to lower or eliminate some of their state income tax or estate tax. Though we can see some similarities between the plans, each one also has its differences. It's important to work with a professional advisor who is well-versed in the plans. It wouldn't hurt to consult with your tax advisor, as well. No matter what steps you take, here are seven tips I like to give when planning for education. Though all have financial implications, not everyone concerns money.

Tip # 1: Help Your Children Hone in on a Career Path

Though it may be difficult at times, paying attention to your children's natural abilities and affinities can help them consider at least a general career field. Math was the only subject I ever liked in school. My dad suggested that I go into the finance field because it dealt with money and I would always be able to find employment because money is universal. I declared Finance as my major as a freshman and never changed my degree. During my junior year of college, I determined I would be a financial advisor.

If your children know what they want to study, they can better search for a school that specializes in that field. This may create an opportunity for your student to find a lower cost school. It may open the door for schools who provide scholarships for a field of study. A strong alumni and internship network can also work wonders for job placement prior to graduation. Research your alma mater (if applicable) to determine if they offer scholarships for alumni's children.

Tip #2: Estimate the Cost

There are many financial calculators that can help determine how much you may need. Research the schools your student may attend and review their tuition history. Remember to factor in an inflation rate for the annual increase in costs.

Tip #3: Set a Specific Goal:
Will You

- Completely pay for education
- Cover half the cost
- Cover tuition
- Cover room & board
- Cover books and lab fees
- Save the same amount for each child

Tip #4: Research Ways to Save for College with a Professional

Search for financial aid and scholarships from various universities. Don't let your child get stuck on a school name. If they want to go to the University of Michigan, but Ohio State University offers them a scholarship, send your children packing to Columbus, Ohio. Search diligently for scholarships at www.myscholly.com. Other ways to save include:

- Savings
- 529 Plans
- Educational Savings Account/Coverdell
- Life Insurance
- Retirement Accounts

Tip #5: Don't Overthink

Just the thought of trying to pay for college can be overwhelming, but don't think so much that you fall victim to analysis paralysis and do nothing. Therefore, it's important to work with professionals. You eat the cost of paying for college just like you eat an elephant—one bite at a time.

Tip #6: Create a Plan That Works for You and Get Started

Review which plan fits best within your goals and budget and get going.

Most plans have very low minimum purchase requirements and maintenance fees. Most allow you to have automatic contributions (some even do payroll deductions). That way, it becomes seamless. Consider using part of your tax refunds toward the plans (if applicable).

Tip #7: Ask Family to Help

Ask your family to consider making contributions into the plan, rather than buying clothes or toys for special occasions, such as:

- Birthdays
- Christmas
- Dedications
- Bar and Bat Mitzvah

There is no cookie-cutter approach to planning for college. You may find that you want to use only one of the plans we discussed, a combination of them, or none at all. What's important is that you develop a plan as soon as possible and seek wise biblical counsel, as we're instructed to. Work that plan. If you find that you can't contribute as much as you would like, don't beat yourself up. No matter what you're able to contribute, your loved one will appreciate it. Also, don't be discouraged by starting small. Small eventually becomes large. Zechariah 4:10 says, *Do not despise these small beginnings, for the Lord rejoices to see the work begin...* Proverbs 13:11 says, *Wealth gained hastily will dwindle, but whoever gathers little by little will increase it*

14 Retirement Planning

Though I wouldn't recommend starting here without reading the other sections, I understand why one may skip forward to this part. Many of us are naturally drawn to subject matters that are either most interesting, most pressing or most concerning. Retirement planning is one of those subjects that likely falls into all three of those categories for many people because it's one of those things you know is coming (hopefully), but you still may be unsure if you're in position to do so. As I sit with people to discuss retirement planning, the most common question I get is, "When can I retire?" or "Do I have enough money saved?" I won't pretend as if those questions are easy to answer. Honestly, I see too many people and financial advisors approaching these items too lightly.

As we go through this section, I want you to remember that the Word of God instructs us to plan, seek wise counsel, use wisdom and not despise small beginnings. So, even if you know you're behind in saving for retirement, don't despair. You'd be surprised what you can accomplish with a plan. There are strategic steps to follow to get results. You may be already doing the steps out of order, and that's okay because you can go back and fill in where you need. No matter where you are in the process, a plan is vital.

Retirement planning has two different phases: accumulation and distribution. Accumulation is typically everything that happens while you're working prior to retirement. During this period, you're trying to get to your "number" that suggests you have enough money to retire and live. Distribution is the second phase. This takes place once you retire and turn the money you've accumulated into an income stream. Arguably, the distribution period may be harder to plan than accumulation because you have no idea how long it will last, nor do you know what all expenses will come in these years. It also can be difficult because you may find yourself caring for an aging parent or spouse. The Distribution phase will be a time of major adjustment. Remember, retirement planning is all about generating income to live without needing to go to work.

When you're working, you're used to getting a check either weekly or bi-weekly. In retirement, you'll have to adjust to receiving things like social security and/or your pension once a month. If you live off dividends and interest, you'll also have to get used to checks where the amounts may vary, and the times you receive those checks will vary. You must determine how much you will distribute from your accounts to avoid running out of money. The normal pattern is to spend more in the early years of retirement and less in the end. That's not always by choice. Some people end up spending so much upfront that they realize, if they don't slow down, they will increase the risk of running out of money. Needless to say, you want to develop a plan prior to retirement. Even if you've already retired, you still want to work with a professional to plan the remainder of your years.

Before we get into the steps of planning your retirement, remember this phrase and say it to yourself as you think and plan: "Retirement planning is about a process, not a product." There are thousands of products to choose from. If you ask many people if they own certain products or accounts, they will tell you they do. However, according to a 2012 study done by the CFP® board of standards, only approximately 31% of people have worked with a professional to develop a plan. Oddly enough, 100% of people desire to retire comfortably but only about 3 in 10 have developed a plan to pursue their retirement goals. So, where's the disconnect? This leads me to conclude that people believe a retirement plan really isn't a written plan as described, but an account, product or publication.

What a Retirement Plan Isn't

Before I explain the importance of a plan and how to develop a retirement plan, please allow me to tell you what a retirement plan is not. A retirement plan is not a 401(K), 403(B), 457 or TSP. Technically, the IRS codes identify them as qualified retirement plans, but stick with my point that they are not retirement plans. These are retirement accounts. If it's a retirement account offered through your company, what's the difference between your 401(K) and your co-worker's? Maybe the option you chose and the balance they have is different. But, for the most part, it's still the same plan. Even if you have an IRA, what makes your IRA different from mine? Balance and investment options may vary. But, for the most part, an IRA is an IRA. What about things like mutual funds, stocks, annuities and ETFs? These products are typically used to fund your retirement accounts. But, on their own, they still wouldn't be considered retirement plans. Even if you're working with a financial advisor, he/she still isn't your plan. I know that may sound silly, but some people approach retirement planning simply based on an advisor's thoughts. But, what happens when your advisor retires, dies or gets fired? Even media outlets, like *The Wall Street Journal* or MSNBC, shouldn't be what you're relying on to get through retirement financially. You may have noticed all the items I listed above are the common items that many of us use surrounding retirement. I want you to recognize all of these have their limits. They are simply tools to put into the retirement tool belt, but they aren't the retirement plan in totality.

What is a Retirement Plan and Why is it Important?

To connect the dots, I like to compare this process to building a home. As you go through the process of selecting a builder and discussing your wishes, one of the earlier things you'll do is go over the blueprints with your builder. Why would blueprints be important if you're working with a builder who has built homes prior to yours? First, your house may be different from your neighbor's house. Likewise, your retirement will be different. Going through the blueprints also allows you to see what will fit in the space you're operating in. While you were building your house, if your builder never drew any blueprints, you'd be concerned. If the builder simply says, "I've been doing this for 25 years, so I don't need blueprints," would that be enough for you? Would you think that was a bit odd, or maybe even lack confidence in what they were building? Even more importantly, is this what you've been doing financially? Are you just going off someone else's experience and expertise, or are you actually taking the time to carefully craft the blueprint to your retirement?

A retirement plan can also be viewed as a compass, roadmap or GPS. Some will point you in the right direction, where one may give you very specific paths to take. Some people retire from one career and enter another. But many people only retire once and, even in the instance where they take a second career, there usually comes a point where they stop working altogether. I use navigational equipment to stress the point that your retirement is likely going to be like a cross-country trip that you've never been on. You pack your bags, load up the RV, pack snacks and set out on your destination. You may have even talked to some people who've been down this road before, but you want to make sure you take all the measures you can to get to your destination as smoothly as possible. Though you've taken some measures to reach your end goal, you know things will likely not go exactly as you planned.

The Importance of a Retirement Plan

In addition to the items previously named, there are two primary reasons that justify having a retirement plan:

1. It's customized to fit your needs.

2. It puts focus on the other five areas of wealth management.

Customization

When I present on retirement planning, that is usually the time when I get the most pushback and eyebrow raises because we've been conditioned to believe things like, a 401(K) is what everyone does for retirement planning. Granted, most do have a 401(K) if the option is available. But, the account in itself isn't a plan. There are very little variances you can make within the plan. Typically, the employer decides which investment company will manage the plan. If you've been with a company long enough, I'm sure you've seen it change. The company, along with the plan administrator, decides what options you have. The company decides how much they'll match (if applicable) and the IRS decides the maximum amount of money you can place into the plan. You don't have much control, other than the investment option you personally choose and how much you can afford to place in your plan.

I'm not suggesting that these types of retirement accounts are bad, but they shouldn't be your sole source of planning as you approach retirement. A retirement plan will take into consideration your concerns, goals and where you are currently financially. There are various publications and suggestions as to how aggressively you should invest and how much you should invest based on age. However, how is that structured to your specific situation? You can have an identical twin sibling, yet have completely different needs and approaches to retirement. You could be aggressive, and your twin conservative. Your twin could be single, while you're married and have children. What if your twin has a pension, and you're a small business owner who has their own 401(K) plan? To achieve your goals, you need a plan built specifically for you.

Other Primary Areas of Financial Planning

As we go through the following primary areas of financial planning, keep in mind that what you do with your money in the left pocket will have an impact on the money in the right pocket. No matter where your money is held, it all touches each other and impacts what you're able to do in other areas of wealth management.

While we have six key areas of financial management, as you approach retirement planning, what have you focused on the most?
It's common for people to focus on one or two areas more than the others. However, to get all the way through retirement, you want to make sure you have all your bases covered.

Suppose that the six areas were equally weighted at 16.67% each. Your primary focus may have been investments and retirement, which is common because the two go hand-in-hand. If this is the case, you're approaching something that you have 100% desired success with only about 33% focus. Only in baseball would 33% be good. Let's discuss why the other areas demand your attention. As you plan your retirement you must consider who the heirs will be to your estate and exactly what they will receive. If you have funds in retirement accounts, once you take the money out, you must consider the tax ramifications of your beneficiary receiving funds, even if it's stretched over their lifetime. Additionally, you would want to make provisions in the instance that you're leaving retirement accounts to a minor. To keep the assets and your information out of probate court, proper estate planning must be used in coordination with your retirement planning.

Many retirees have saved a large portion in retirement accounts that are taxable upon distribution. The IRS requires you to take a portion of your retirement account out from age 70 ½ and each year beyond that. However, what happens if you ever realize you won't need all the funds in your retirement account? Imagine that you're 75. You won't turn 76 until next year and you have $1,000,000 in a traditional IRA. The IRS's required minimum distribution would force you to take out roughly $43,668, which I will remind you again is 100% taxable. With your additional income, this may push you into a higher tax bracket. Do you really want your relatives (unless it's your surviving spouse) to really inherit $1,000,000 that will be taxable at all times? Not only will they have to pay income taxes on this money, but if your net worth is high enough, your estate may also be subject to a death tax. What if there was a way that you could've prepared ahead of time to either lessen the tax bill or completely remove it?

In addition to including a proper estate plan into your retirement planning, you also must consider insurance planning. Medical costs are the most unpredictable to estimate and will likely be one of the largest expenses for most retirees. Additionally, you must consider what type of treatment you may need based on your current health, as well as your family history. If you're relatively healthy, and you come from a family where longevity is common, you must consider if it makes sense to purchase a long-term care policy. Many couples have worked hard to save for retirement. One person could go into a nursing home and use practically all the money that was saved jointly for a long retirement. Of course, saving for retirement is to make sure you have what you need and not run out of money. However, I'm pretty sure if there was an opportunity to leave a financial legacy to someone you love, you would want to do that. But, if your insurance planning doesn't coordinate with retirement planning, you may forfeit the opportunity to do that.

Insurance also comes into play if you have a situation such as mine. My wife has made the wonderful, sacrificial task of staying at home with our children. So, my wife's ability to save for retirement is going to be solely based on my ability to work and earn money. If I were to come down with some sort of disease, or was involved in an accident and became disabled, my wife now has lost her ability to save and plan for her retirement. On the other hand, if I made sure I had a proper disability insurance plan in place, and something like the former were to happen, I would be more likely to be able to continue to plan and invest for retirement, even if I couldn't work. This same scenario also comes into question if I were to unfortunately pass away suddenly. Not only would our household income diminish to take care of our immediate needs, but it would be forever altered. I would also need to make sure I carry proper life insurance.

Your scenario will likely not be the same as mine, but your insurance needs must be considered as you consider your long-term goals. I've run across several situations where someone dies, and they still owe money on their home. The only asset that was left behind was a 401(K) or IRA. Now, their loved ones are faced with the undesired position where they either must sell a home, use cash on hand, or pull money from an IRA and pay taxes on money they didn't anticipate using right away. This becomes especially true if you're a small business owner. Not only are you responsible for your business, but your family and any employees you may have. If you aren't physically well, chances are the business will not be financially well. You are the business. So, if the business can't continue, you may have to sell or close the business, causing employees to lose their jobs.

For some people, they are what you would call "401(K) poor." If you removed their retirement accounts from the equation, they may not have any other liquid assets to use. In these scenarios, I find that people put themselves in a "Catch 22" scenario because they don't want to risk losing money because it may be all they have. But, because it's all they have, it puts more pressure on those funds to grow. You can't afford to take risks, but then you can't afford to *not* take risks. As you develop retirement plans, you also would consider your investment mix in both the accumulation and distribution phases.

Lastly, and probably the most obvious connection to retirement planning, are your investments. Remember, retirement planning is about a process, not a product. If your retirement plan is the engine that drives the car, the products are the gas that go into the car. Join me in an experiment with a friend or relative who you know has investments and ask them a few questions:

1. How did you go about picking the investments you own?

2. Why do you invest the way you do?

3. How do you know you're making the right decision?

I'm confident if you ask enough people, you'll likely hear answers for the first question to be, "I looked at a rating." "I looked at the options I was given and chose the best performers." "It's what a friend, relative, co-worker or advisor told me to do." For question two, you may get responses such as, "I was told based on my age this is how people should invest." "I'm conservative, moderate or aggressive." "This is how Mom and Dad taught me to invest." Number three may be the question that stumps them, but a likely response will still be something along the lines of, "I trust my advisor to give me good advice." "I have historical investment experience," or they may be honest with you and tell you they aren't sure. Many tend to take the mindset of whatever they can accumulate will determine how they live, which is completely backwards. Your goals and plans for retirement should determine how you invest.

There was a familiar commercial of an investment company that asked, "What's your number?" It's a legitimate question, which asks how much money you will need for retirement. It's hard to hit a target you're not aiming for. Without knowing how much you need for retirement, you may find it difficult to develop an investment plan. Embedded in knowing your number is not only choosing the right investments to get you to that number, but it also displays how much of a return you may need to get to that number, which would also illustrate the proper amount of risk you need to assume. Again, all these things are illustrations, not the Ten Commandments. Imagine that you require a 7% average return to achieve your retirement goals. Then, you would only need to assume the amount of risk that comes with that type of investment. For example, let's say that a portfolio that has consistently given a 7% return has never gone down more than 15%. The most you could lose is 15%. Why would you then invest in the portfolio that gives a 10% upside, but you could also lose 25%? That's not to say your 7% average return portfolio won't grow beyond 7% in any given year, but why take on additional and unnecessary risk? From the people who I've worked with over the years, I've found far more are taking on too much risk than not enough. The numbers aren't even close to being equal. You don't lead your retirement goals with investments. You pursue your retirement goals with a retirement plan, and investments should follow them.

The Retirement Planning Process

Again, retirement planning is not about a product. It's all about the process. Hopefully by now, you've bought into the idea that a mutual fund or annuity is not the key to your financial stability. The plans you put into action that may just use one of those products we've discussed throughout are the key. If you're still a bit skeptical, let's at least agree that we know what a retirement plan is and is not, and we know why having a formal plan is important. Even if you're still trying to wrap your head around the items we've discussed up to this point, worry not because I'm going to give you the six-step process to creating your own retirement plan. If you recall from the beginning of the book we talked about the 6 key areas of wealth management. As you will soon learn, there is a process within the process when it comes to retirement planning.

The Six Steps to Creating a Retirement Plan:

1. Picking a Financial Advisor
2. Define and Establish Your Goals
3. Analyzing & Review
4. Recommendation
5. Plan Implementation
6. Monitor, Review and Adjust.

Step 1: Picking a Financial Advisor
Why do you start with the advisor?

The old saying states, "It's not how you start, but how you finish." But, when it comes to your retirement, how you start will have a large effect on how you finish. If you haven't started the way you've hoped, I don't want to discourage you. But starting correctly can help you end correctly. If you are part of the group who hasn't embraced this first step, you do have the ability to go back and correct it.

Contrary to what you may have read or thought, developing a financial plan starts with selecting a financial advisor that will help you develop these plans. One of the major reasons you want to start with a financial advisor is because there is a different view the advisor will likely bring to your goals. Consider the following example. I assume you're like most people and enjoy a clean home. Whether your home is cleaned on a daily, weekly or even a monthly basis, it still gets cleaned. Because your home is cleaned on a regular basis with a certain style, you can say at any given time, "My home is clean." Now, imagine after 1, 3, 5, 10 or even 20 years, you bring someone else in your home to either help you clean, do the cleaning for you, or assess your ability to clean. This "assessor of cleanliness" will have the ability to view things with fresh eyes that you've never seen before. You may forget to dust, clean the blinds, wash the windows or clean underneath the refrigerator. Your new hired cleaning staff may also affirm the work you've done and give you suggestions on how to work smarter, not harder. Instead of risking your life by reaching from the top of a chair on your tippy-toes to clean your ceiling fan, your new cleaning person suggests an extension rod to make the cleaning easier and safer. I know this is a simplistic example, but it shows the value an advisor potentially delivers.

You may not know as much as you either think or hope to know concerning financial management. There is value in talking through your ideas and goals with someone who has an education and experience within the field.

Whatever profession you come from, it will be nearly impossible for me to fill your shoes. I don't have your education, experience and expertise, nor the passion for what you do. Take this same position and apply it to your finances. Imagine that you must have heart surgery, and you must pick from three different surgeons. Surgeon number 1 has no experience as a surgeon but has read a few books and articles. Surgeon number 2 has a bit more information and some experience with cardiology, but really isn't a cardiologist. They're actually a sports writer who has a "passion" for hearts and does surgery on the side in their spare time. Lastly, surgeon number 3 loved science from a young age, received a bachelor's degree in Pre-Med, went on to graduate from medical school, and now has been performing heart surgery for 10 years. Who would you choose? Undoubtedly, you would pick surgeon number 3, unless you're just a thrill seeker.

But there's a fourth surgeon who has been there from day 1: *you*. Many companies seek to convince you daily that, with a template, a questionnaire, a phone call, you can do it yourself. This isn't just a matter of experience, knowledge and passion; it's also a matter of time.

Using the same example of the cardiologist, imagine you still need heart surgery. You discover the template, purchase the tools, and go home and perform the surgery yourself. Could you be successful? Absolutely! But is it likely that success will be achieved? Probably not. The same precision required for your surgery is the same precision you need for your retirement.

Some companies will market how much money you will save over the years by doing it yourself. This may be true, but the old saying is, "You get what you pay for." Another aspect of this as it relates to your money is this: will it cost you more to have an advisor, or is the greater cost not having an advisor? Oftentimes, we don't consider the "cost" for what we pay. According to Zig Ziglar, what you pay refers to the either one-time or ongoing fee you're giving your advisor. The "cost" is the long-term effect of having the advisor serve as your retirement dream advocate. Therefore, it's important not to make decisions (especially related to your retirement) solely based on price. I'm not saying price isn't important. But it shouldn't be the most important.

I know advisors can get a bad reputation because of the shortcomings of other advisors. But many of them have built a practice on honesty, integrity and helping people achieve their goals.

Your advisor may be able to help you mitigate or avoid losses, save you money on your taxes and help you make rational decisions. It's a proven psychological fact that we make decisions emotionally and justify them rationally. Using the same approach with money can be detrimental to your financial goals. There's also a long-term cost with you managing your own retirement. You may have peace knowing you're in control and that you're not being "ripped off" by any shady advisor. But you must also acknowledge where you fall short. Financial literacy isn't typically taught in schools. Therefore, many of us have limited knowledge concerning money. Yet, we make financial decisions daily. I think we've all had moments in our financial lives where we can look back and realize, had we known better, we likely wouldn't make the same decision again. This may be true for you as it relates to retirement and investment decisions. You must come to grips with the fact that when you're managing your own retirement, at some point, you may make a decision the same way. This could "cost" you money and the retirement lifestyle you desire. There is something that can't often be measured that an advisor can provide you; Objectivity. We are emotional people, and many times we make decisions that aren't in our best interest because it was rooted in emotion. Your advisor has no emotional ties to your money, which doesn't mean they don't care, but they shouldn't be swayed by feelings.

Lastly, your advisor would be a source of financial accountability. What happens when we start to make decisions they don't align with our financial goals? If we don't have someone there to pull us back, we could go down a long spiral that derails everything. By now, I hope you're convinced why step number 1 is important. Even still, you may be unsure of how one selects a financial advisor.

We're careful when it comes to picking a house, a job or career. One could argue the selection of an advisor is even more important. One of the main "nuggets" I want you to pick up on is the fact that there's no perfect way to select a financial advisor. Since it's your financial future, you must approach it the best way you see fit. Take your time and be very active in this process. Too often people rely on others to make their selection for them. Although the journey to selecting an advisor does involve others at times, in the end, it's your retirement, your life, your money and your choice.

For some, it's a matter of experience in the financial field. Some people seek an advisor who has been through the ups and downs of the market because they have helped their clients navigate through tough waters. Relative to experience is also education. Some clients not only review their advisor's experience, but they also examine the advisor's education. Some clients want to work with advisors who have degrees in the financial field. Whether it's business management, finance, insurance or economics, studying the field prior to working in the field may be important to you, as well.

What goes hand-in-hand with both experience and education is professional designations and certifications. I will caution you ahead of time that none of these items guarantee success. But an advisor with a professional designation does suggest that the advisor has experience beyond the requirement of their field. Though some financial planning companies desire, or even require, their advisors to hold certifications, the majority of the certifications are voluntary. I hold a Certified Financial Planner™ designation. This wasn't anything my company (at the time) made me do, or even encouraged me to do. I chose to put myself through the grueling process to give myself the ability to look at each client's "big picture" concerning their finances. Some of the designations may also indicate a specialized area of work for the advisor.

Another area of consideration could be your advisor's age. This may be surprising to you, and I don't encourage discrimination of any sort. But there are times where experience and age matters. However, that doesn't guarantee your success. Some clients work with new advisors and things go well. Other times, clients work with advisors who have 30 years of experience and still lose money. Working with a younger advisor could also bring fresh eyes and ideas to your financial planning experience. Also, consider how long you anticipate your retirement will be. Will it be 20, 25 or 30 years? I've yet to meet a client that entered retirement with the intention of making it short. So, also consider the likelihood that your advisor would be around through the tenure of your retirement.

Also consider what company the advisor works for. Some clients prefer to work with "bigger" named companies because they think bigger is better. Some peoples also prefer to work with companies that are independent and offer investment products from various companies

When you're dealing with companies that create the investment they recommend, there could be a conflict of interest, even when it's unintended. If I own a mutual fund, and the mutual fund I own matches your needs, naturally, I would prefer you to buy my fund. But that also may keep me from doing my due diligence to make sure it's the best fit. Another issue with the investment advisor and company being the same may be the possibility that I only can offer my own company's investments. This may be a red flag because you may not be able to assess if what you're doing is in your best interest. You may not know if the company even offers what you need to help pursue your goals.

One of the most common ways you can pursue a relationship with a financial advisor is through recommendations. Those recommendations can come from relatives, co-workers, friends or even parishioners. When seeking a recommendation from someone, consider someone who you believe is wise with money and trustworthy. As you approach this recommendation, be sure to ask the person referring if they're happy with the relationship and if they would recommend them. Don't base the person's happiness solely on returns. If you've invested long enough, you may have experienced some loss. Happiness is subjective. So, whether they tell you they're happy or not, make sure you understand why.

You can also do your own research or set your own criteria. Some advisors specialize in working with executives, small business owners and doctors. However, other advisors only deal with areas like insurance or the financial plan itself. You can search for advisors who either have an office close to your home or work address. There are a couple of other tools you can use either on their own, or in conjunction with everything else. If you desire to work with a Certified Financial Planner™ you can access a list of advisors on cfp.net and search under "Find a professional?" Their database not only gives you a list based on proximity, but you also can view each advisor's specialized areas of focus, how long they've been certified, if they've had any bankruptcy, if they have a minimum required investment amount, and how they're compensated, amongst many other things. Another valuable tool is http://www.finra.org/ "Broker Check." According to their website, FINRA stands for the Financial Industry Regulatory Authority.

FINRA is the first line of oversight for broker-dealers and, through its comprehensive regulatory programs, regulates both the firms and professionals that sell securities in the United States and the U.S. securities markets. FINRA oversees more than 3,955 brokerage firms, 162,650 branch offices and 643,320 registered securities representatives. FINRA touches virtually every aspect of the securities business – from registering industry participants to examining securities firms; writing rules and enforcing those rules and the federal securities laws; informing and educating the investing public; providing trade reporting and other industry utilities; and administering the largest dispute resolution forum for investors, firms and individual brokers.

Broker check allows you to view your prospective advisor's professional work history, learn how long the advisor has been in the business (licensed), and previous firms they've worked with. Broker check also shows the investment license/s they hold, what states they're registered to do business in, as well as any previous customer complaints or judgments against the advisor. A client complaint is a serious matter. However, there are some instances where the complaint could either be an exaggeration of events, or outright unfounded. On the flip side, an advisor who doesn't have *any* client complaints doesn't guarantee that there's no possibility of a negative event regarding your interaction with them. For example, take the now infamous Bernard (Bernie) Madoff. Mr. Madoff had previously worked in the industry for 40 plus years with no reported infractions. Yet, we know what the end result was.

All the above-mentioned items are tools. However, they can't be the end all be all to your advisor relationship. Sometimes it's good to use old-fashioned intuition. One of the biggest issues I see is that clients sometimes simply don't ask enough questions. Sometimes it's a fear of sounding "silly" and not being understood. You should still ask your questions. Continue to ask until you receive answers you're satisfied with. The satisfaction of the answers may not necessarily mean hearing what you want. But did the advisor answer your question directly, or did they beat around the bush? Since you're essentially handing your future over to them, no advisor should take offense to you asking them questions, no matter how many it may be. You don't want to leave anything on the table that would prevent you from making an educated decision and giving you comfort with that decision. As you pursue this important decision, don't forget to seek the Lord. As with any decision, prayer should be a major component.

There are a lot of advisors out here, so keep searching until you find who you're comfortable working with. There is no perfect way to find the perfect financial advisor. But, as you search, there are questions you should ask, but may not know to ask. I wouldn't recommend rolling out all these questions at once. However, here are 25 questions to consider asking an advisor before and after you give them your money. Choose your top five or go for all 25.

1. **What is your investment philosophy and approach to financial planning?**

You'll want to know if their outlook on money management matches your beliefs and convictions. You'll also learn the "how" behind their operation. It doesn't mean things have to be 100% the same, but there may be certain items that are deal breakers to you.

2. **Are you a fiduciary?**

You'll want to know what requirements of care and disclosures the advisor and the investment company has to you and their other clients. You'll also learn if they have requirements to act in your best interest as they give you financial advice.

3. **What is your educational background, and do you have any professional designations and licenses?**

This question will give you insight into the advisor's education, as well as the areas of financial planning your advisor is licensed to give advice in. This is important because the term "financial advisor" has become watered down. There are many people who profess to be advisors and have no education or license to back up the claim. Some firms encourage professional designations like the CFP®, CFA®, ChFC®, CEPA. However, very few require them, which means most advisors have gone out of their way to obtain and maintain these designations. Through classroom study time, exams, and continuing education requirements; thousands of dollars and hours are invested.

4. **What is your professional experience?**

This allows you to learn more about the advisor's career and how that experience relates to the services you seek. If they hold professional licensing or certifications, this information can be verified through the various governing bodies.

5. **How are you paid and how much do you typically charge?**

Though fees vary by the nature of the relationship, advisors and firms usually have a range of fees they charge. Sometimes, there may be a minimum fee.

6. **What types of services do you provide?**

You'll learn the advisor's area/s of expertise, as well as the advisor's limitations. Do they have the capabilities to handle some or all your financial needs?

7. **What does your typical client look like?**

Some advisors specialize in working with small business owners, executives, retirees or clients who only have a particular net worth. Some advisors may only work with clients of certain ages or professions, as well. This will give you some insight on whether you're interviewing the right advisor.

8. **How often do you typically contact your clients?**

There should be some expectation of how often you will speak and/or meet with your advisor.

9. **Will we only work with you?**

You should know whether your prospective advisor works alone or takes a team approach to delivering their services. You should also know whether the person you originally speak with will be the person overseeing your finances. I know that may seem weird, but some places are set up in this manner.

10. **Why should I do business with you?**

This may be the most difficult question to answer from the advisor's perspective. What you want to know is what sets your perspective or current advisor apart from every other advisor, and how that directly relates to your goal. If you're an experienced investor, or you consider yourself financially astute, this also answers the question of why the advisor may be able to better handle your money than you.

11. Can you show me a sample of a financial plan?

If you're seeking an advisor for an actual written financial plan, ask them to show you a sample of what their planning process looks like.

12. What are your typical office hours?

This may seem like a goofy question, but this allows you to learn how accessible your advisor is, especially if there's an emergency.

13. How quickly do you respond to emails and/or phone calls?

Again, this may seem like another silly question, but various surveys given to clients often show the number one thing that leads to dissatisfaction is the time it takes for the advisor to get back to them.

14. What other areas do you service?

If you're a snow bird, or someone who lives and works in various locations, you should know if your advisor can accommodate your needs.

15. Do you have a backup if you're unavailable?

Whether it's a vacation, sickness or emergency on the advisor's end, it's always great to know that plans have been put in place to service your needs should the advisor not be able to respond.

16. Do you own your book of business?

In the event your advisor leaves their company, you would want to know the ease of maintaining your relationship with your advisor.

17. How long do you plan on working in the industry?

One may be inclined to work with an advisor whose time frame in the industry matches your investment time frame. In some instances, it matches the length of time you anticipate you may need their services. You should also know how the advisor will handle events like retirement and death, and how you would be impacted.

18. **Do you have a professional mentor, or have you had one in the past?**

This not only touches on experience, but also how much the advisor may value others' opinions and experience, or if they believe they have it all figured out. Mentors have also helped many advisors become advisors. If you deal with one who has ever had a mentor, they will tell you it's made the difference in them becoming successful.

19. **Why did you choose this profession/what keeps you here?**

This should tell what motivates your advisor.

20. **How does your life and family life mix?**

There's no harm in knowing what your advisor personally values, how those things rank in their life, and how they find balance in each one.

21. **Do you take part in any charitable organizations for your profession?**

This gives you an idea of how the advisor views their profession on a "big picture" scale. Do they take part in anything where they aren't paid?

22. **How will my family be included in the planning process?**

Some advisors prefer to only deal with the owner of the investment account, while others may require, if someone is married, that both parties be involved in the process. If seniors are involved, this may be an adult child, as well.

23. **What do you believe to be the most important aspect of financial planning?**

You'll learn the driving force behind their practice and what they tend to focus on. This may also reveal a bias that some of us may have.

24. **Have you ever been disciplined in your career?**

This goes without question, but you want to know if the advisor has been fired from previous firms, involved in client disputes, or if they've had any of their licenses suspended or revoked.

25. **What do you look for in a client?**

You'll know what the ideal client looks like for the advisor, not just from a financial aspect, but what they want in a client/advisor relationship.

These questions aren't a full exhaustive questionnaire. But you can pick out what's most relevant for you and go from there. Make sure you understand the advisor and the advisor understands you. Once you've selected your advisor, the next action would be to define and establish your goals.

Step 2: Define & Establish Your Goals

The second step in creating a comprehensive retirement plan is to define and establish your goals. On the surface, defining and establishing goals may seem to be a matter of semantics. But there is a difference between the two.

Defining and establishing goals, takes your goals and quantifies them. A comfortable retirement, for you, may be your current gross income on an after-tax basis. If you make $100,000 per year, and your net income is $75,000 per year, your goal may be a retirement income of $75,000 through your retirement years. Quantifying what type of income makes you comfortable allows you to establish (comfortable) your goals and define ($75,000 per year) them. For people who desire to travel, that goal still needs to be defined and established. At what point do you want to travel? Where do you want to travel? How often do you want to travel? Once we can answer these questions surrounding retirement travel, we can quantify that and figure out how much money you'll need each year for travel.

Everything you do in retirement is going to surround money. Whether it's coming in or going out, you need money. To make sure you have the money you'll need to achieve your goals, you need a retirement budget.

A retirement budget also allows you to categorize each item so money isn't disappearing from you. The biggest benefit that I believe comes from a budget is to prevent you from overspending, especially in the early years of retirement which in turn puts more stress on your assets to grow. This may provide liberty in other areas, especially for newer retirees. Many publications from various news outlets and investment companies take polls and track spending from retirees. These publications suggest retirees tend to spend more money during their first 5-10 years within retirement than any other period. I think the reason why is three-fold:

1. **A lack of a retirement budget:**

    I believe it's the sheer excitement from exiting the work world and more free time. Some people worked six or seven days a week for long periods. They simply didn't have time to spend their money. You combine free time, excitement and little restraint, it's easy to see how money can quickly flow out. Some people didn't follow budgets prior to retirement, so having one for retirement can sometimes be a challenge.

2. **Reality checks:**

    When you start to travel and have fun in retirement without a budget, the money tends to go quicker. Oddly enough, one of the biggest struggles people have expressed to me is going from weekly or bi-weekly checks to one check a month. Without having much experience with one check, overspending can become imminent. Once the money starts to flow out faster than retirees expect, they sometimes pull back from some of the activities they were doing when they worked. They adjust goals because they realize, at the pace they're spending money, their retirement money could be cut short quickly.

3. **Age:**

    This may not be true for all retirees, but for some, there are certain mobility restrictions that come with growing older. Even if it's not mental, the physical aspect of retirement does change your lifestyle. You may not golf as much at 75 as you did at 66. At 80, you may not be able to hit the slopes like you did at 50. Even if you physically can do all the things you enjoyed through retirement, you just may not want to, which is your choice.

Another aspect of aging through retirement is your goal to leave an inheritance for your family, church or favorite charity. You may be surprised how many times people have told me, "I don't want to spend the kids' inheritance." The interesting part is we weren't discussing buying a Bentley, just doing basic repairs on their home. But, at certain ages, people seem to start to think less about retirement and more about estate planning.

Overspending doesn't discriminate. Some people say, "I'm different" or "That won't happen to me." But, what if it does? While you have the chance, let's consider what goes into creating a retirement budget.

Expenses That Will Go Away

As you create a retirement budget (especially if done before retirement), think about what expenses will be eliminated once you retire. For many people, the biggest goal approaching retirement outside of amassing large sums of money is debt elimination. The biggest debt most of us will carry in our lifetime is the mortgage on our home/s. Though carrying debt into retirement has unfortunately become more common today, the goal has typically been to have your home paid off before retirement. Usually, your mortgage is likely the most common and largest expense that goes away (hopefully). Depending on your occupation, there may be various expenses associated with work that you won't need to pay anymore. It could be uniforms or professional dues for associations or clubs that you may either decrease your activity with or outright end.

Expenses That Will Be Added

As some expenses will disappear, there are also expenses that will come into the equation once retirement starts. There is a greater likelihood that medical expenses will increase and could be in the form of larger premiums, larger deductibles or Medicare coverages that you'll need to ensure you have the proper insurance coverage. We've already discussed the travel budget, but I want to touch on it again because this needs to be a defined number. Saying, "I want to travel" just isn't enough. If you've waited to purchase long-term care insurance until retirement, not only does this have to be included in the budget, but it may be difficult to calculate because of the ever-changing nature of long-term care insurance. Some people's retirement plan may also include selling a primary residence and moving. If you use the cash from the home to purchase a condo, you'll still have association dues, which is an added expense. If you decide to sell your home and move into an apartment, you obviously have rent that needs to be included in your retirement budget. Some also move into senior living facilities or assisted living/nursing homes. As you know, these can be budget busters. There will be other considerations that aren't mentioned in this book because they're based on your lifestyle, which may or may not apply to other people's goals.

Expenses That Will Remain, but Change Over Time

I've still yet to figure out how to eliminate all expenses. So, let's consider the expenses that will likely remain, but increase over time. Even if nothing else changes during your retirement years (which is highly unlikely), history tells us the cost of living makes basic living more expensive every year. Some will even go as far as to say that because interest rates have been at historical lows, inflation is negated. However, many retirees would seem to suggest that it's a bit harder to maintain and live the same way than in previous years.

There are certain activities around the house that you've found much joy in doing over the years. But, as you get further into retirement, you may not have the time, energy or physical capacity to perform. Things like cleaning gutters, cutting grass, as well as clearing snow may be an added expense to your budget.

Until recent changes, the cost of fuel for a car has become increasingly more expensive over the years, even if you're driving less. For those who live in the Midwest or other areas that get cold temperatures, one of the areas of concern each year for retirees is the cost to heat homes. Depending on the size and age of the home, it's easy to see a $300 heating bill during the winter months. That's just one utility. We've already touched on healthcare but consider the worst-case scenario possible and place an annual increase on that cost within your retirement budget. The same goes for food.

Step 3: Data Gathering & Analyzing

Each part of the retirement planning process is important and shouldn't be skipped or overlooked. Yes, picking an advisor and setting goals are very important, but everything you do to pursue those goals is going to be based on this step. This is also a very invasive step where you're allowing someone to take a microscopic look inside your life. That's right; a stranger is being allowed access to some of the most intimate and private information about you and your family, but it's necessary for the process to work. Whatever you put into this retirement planning step will determine what comes out. No matter what effort you've put into the preceding and proceeding steps, if you don't get this part right, everything else will be off. If you put junk in, you can expect junk to come out.

Building trust and comfort with an advisor comes over time; but if you give your advisor incorrect or incomplete information, the end result will be an incorrect or incomplete retirement plan. I can recount several times where people approached me to assist with a financial need, but they wouldn't release key information during our conversation and I had to decline working with them. I often use the analogy of visiting a doctor. Before the doctor gives recommendations or provides prescriptions, your doctor will ask questions concerning your health history, the reason for the visit, allergies, and what prescriptions you may already take. You don't have to be a doctor to know that mixing the wrong medications could be fatal –the same is true financially. Not only that, but the industry has a rule called "KYC" or Know Your Customer, which means there is a standard process for collecting information to support financial recommendations as an advisor. It's a risk for both you and the advisor to act on incomplete or incorrect information. So, make sure you give as much information as your advisor needs.

This is the most labor-intensive part for you, but it's also the most critical. It may take some time to gather all the information. Therefore, I send new clients a checklist, so they can prepare to gather documents ahead of time. The exact items required will depend on what services you're employing your advisor to assist you with, but here are some basics:

<u>Social Security statements</u> that illustrate your estimated benefits at various ages. For years, Social Security would send these out every year, but as of late they seem to be moving more towards an online account. The good thing about setting up an online account is it allows you to instantly download your report from ssa.gov.

<u>Estimated pension benefit</u> if you qualify for a pension. Much like your Social Security statement, the pension estimator illustrates various income options based on age, but they also display your various income amounts based on any applicable beneficiary options. This may seem pretty straight forward, but I've seen people make mistakes in electing their pension benefits because they don't understand what the definitions mean.

The most important takeaway is this. Social security and pension elections are figuratively and literally million-dollar decisions that you get to make once. Don't make that decision without professional help.

Statements

Statement gathering as it relates to retirement planning tells the full picture of where you are financially and will also clarify any misunderstandings you may have regarding the investments you own. Outside of traditional stock holdings, very few people I've worked with have correctly explained their investment holdings, especially if they have more than one. I've also discovered that, over time, some clients' portfolios haven't matched their description, general investment philosophy, or comfort level. I've lost count of how many people have told me, "I'm conservative" and their investment holdings are anything but conservative. Many times, people believe the number of investment accounts, positions, and locations equals diversification, and that's not always the case. For instance, if you have S&P 500 index funds at Vanguard, Fidelity, and JP Morgan, though these are different investment companies and managers, the investments are essentially the same. The statements allow your advisor to look at your assets and see if they're truly diversified, or you just have money in different places. This allows your advisors to spot overlaps as in our above scenario and reallocate your holdings to asset classes that may be underutilized or missing in your portfolio.

Once all the statements are gathered, which again may take some time, it's on the advisor to take what they've been given and analyze the information. Most advisors these days use financial planning software to put the big picture on paper and view the following items.

Are Your Goals Achievable?

The first part in the analyzing portion of the retirement planning process is to determine if the goals set forth in step 2 are achievable. If they aren't achievable, we would have to re-assess and prioritize the goals to see if some need to be lowered or eliminated. If goals aren't achievable in the current scenario, some considerations may be to extend work years, contribute more to retirement accounts, work part-time in retirement, or lower the amount of money you will live on amongst other things.

Will You Run Out of Money?

For most people, the million-dollar question related to retirement planning is: Do I have enough money to last for my retirement? There are many economic and individual considerations that go into answering this question, but planning can help answer this question. The assumptions included in this portion consider your income, assets, how long you have until retirement, retirement contribution amounts, health, family longevity history, estimated time in retirement and many other things. Investment return assumptions are also included in the mix based on the risk tolerance and portfolio construction.

Running out of money may also be a result of an unrealistic lifestyle. I recall a scenario where a potential client had a portfolio of about $800,000 which is no small sum, but they wanted to take part of the money to buy a new home and withdraw $80,000 a year from the portfolio. You don't need any fancy calculation to see this isn't reasonable. Even if the home purchase wasn't an option, $80,000 from the portfolio would be gone in 10 years if no growth were seen on the accounts.

Proper Levels of Insurance

Another consideration during the analyzing section of the financial planning process is maintaining the proper levels of insurance. Proper levels of insurance will be relative to individual needs, but during this time an advisor would typically consider life, disability, long-term care insurance, and others. This is another time where financial planning software is important because what may seem like "enough" to the naked eye might be inadequate once you consider things like inflation and worst-case scenarios. When allowing for levels of life insurance, you must consider not only your health, but the health of your dependents. Once everything is reviewed and analyzed, then you can move on to the most exciting part for you and your advisor: the recommendations.

Step 4: Recommendations

As a planner, I always get excited when I reach this step because I now can show people on paper what's needed to appropriately pursue their goals. This is the time where all the thoughts, dreams, and hard work come to life. Many times, this takes a lot of changing, which may be frightening.

Income Strategies

Another common misstep I see when dealing with people is a lack of a clear income strategy, which may seem unfathomable because income is what you need in retirement. Some advisors talk in products and returns, but as you approach retirement you need to talk in cash flow. As I just described, one of the first considerations is how and when to draw pensions and Social Security. Up until recently, this step could get a little bit more complex for married couples; nonetheless, there are other considerations in drawing Social Security.

If you collect before your full retirement age, you will not only have a permanent reduction in your benefits, but you could also end up getting less money as result of a possible penalty from Social Security for working while collecting Social Security. If you are in good health and continue to work past full retirement age, or you just delay taking your Social Security, you're able to get an 8% simple interest increase in your benefit between full retirement age and 70.

For those who've been divorced, collecting Social Security also presents different opportunities and choices.

Additional considerations are also available for widows and widowers. Typically, the earliest you can draw Social Security retirement benefits is 62, but if you're a widow/widower you could potentially draw a survivor's retirement benefit as early as 60.

As we described in the analyzing portion, if you have a pension, how you collect that pension needs to be considered not only from the withdrawal benefits options, but as it relates to your Social Security and other assets. As we discussed earlier, this is another way that people have used their permanent life insurance policy to supplement retirement needs.

Withdrawal Strategies

Withdrawal strategies should be considered together with income strategies. Where income strategies help determine how to receive your income, withdrawal strategies determine where to get the income from. For many people, their pension and Social Security may not provide enough income to meet their needs, so you must consider where else you can possibly go for income. This is one of the crucial parts about reviewing investment strategies as you approach and start retirement. But, more importantly, you want to know your assets will produce income for you. Withdrawal strategies not only consider where to draw income, but also how much and how often. Many financial publications suggest a 4% withdrawal rate from portfolio assets, but you may be able to take higher amounts from certain assets. For example, if you have an annuity that guarantees you a 5% withdrawal rate for life, you could possibly take the max from the annuity and avoid drawing down other assets you may want to maintain.

Additionally, as you determine where to draw assets from, you also want to consider if those assets already produce income or need to be repositioned to income producing assets. For example, if you own all growth mutual funds, keep in mind that these funds probably pay very little dividend if any, so much of your income may be based on market performance which, of course, fluctuates. Now, imagine if you took those same assets and kept part of them in the growth funds to try and keep pace with inflation, and then moved another portion into bonds, preferred or dividends stocks, and other assets that produce income. Though these assets will still fluctuate in value, the income you need may still be generated in volatile markets.

Within all the withdrawal strategies that I haven't touched on to this point are income taxes. Part of the reason why ROTH accounts, whether IRA or

401(K), are so popular is the fact that taxes are a concern for many people. Taxes are one of the conundrums we will face in retirement because we can plan all we want to have tax strategies, but they're all based on assumptions and none of us know what the tax codes will be in the future. Your Social Security and pensions may be fully taxable, but depending on your total income, your dividends from certain stocks and stock mutual funds may be only taxed at 15% or not taxed at all. Essentially you could potentially receive tax free or tax-reduced income from stock or mutual fund portfolios in non-retirement accounts during your retirement years.

If you're pulling income from an annuity that wasn't a retirement account, you're taxed on gains first, so this means all the money you pull from the annuity is taxed at your normal tax rates until you remove all the gains. If you purchased an annuity for $100,000 and over the years it grew to $200,000, once you begin to take income from that annuity, you must pay taxes on all of your withdrawals until you have removed all your gains and gotten back down to your initial investment. Obviously, assets pulled from traditional IRA, SEP, SIMPLE, 401(K) are fully taxable, so you must be very careful with your retirement income strategy, not just from a standpoint of depleting your assets, but also from a taxation standpoint. One of the best things you can do, if your income allows, is to try to have assets that have different tax treatment, so you can have options. If you retire with a large sum of taxable assets and tax rates are low in your retirement, you might want to consider pulling money from the taxable assets first because you may pay lower tax rates. On the other side of the coin, if you have been able to save money in tax-free accounts and upon retirement tax rates are higher, it may make sense to pull from those tax-free assets first if your circumstances allow. As you move through the 6 areas of wealth management, it's key that you have a balance of assets as it relates to taxes. You want to have assets that are taxed now, taxed deferred, and tax free.

Investment Recommendations

Not only should your investments match your needs, but they should make sense to you. I know this may seem elementary, but you'd be surprised how many people don't understand what they own. I don't expect you to regurgitate every investment objective for every fund you own, but you should have some general idea of what you're investing in and why, especially from a risk standpoint. The 2008 market collapse was an unfortunate wake-up call for many investors who thought they were in conservative, low-risk investment, only to find their accounts down 20%. A lot of factors contributed to 2008 and I'm sensitive to what happened in people's lives because I know it wasn't easy to deal with personally or professionally, but some of those losses can be attributed to us having too much confidence in the markets and our advisors and not enough focus on understanding what we own. I know it may seem like I'm beating a dead horse and that isn't my intention. If you don't get anything else from this book, please understand that your investments should be constructed in a way that you understand and are best positioned to achieve your financial goals, not just to get higher "returns."

One of the major decisions within the recommendation steps is determining how and where to invest your assets. Some other assets that are often considered in the recommendations are:

- Banks- CD's, money market, savings
- Stocks
- Mutual Funds
- Annuities
- Real Estate – whether mutual funds, rental properties, flips, & commercial properties
- Exchange Traded Funds
- Commodities – Gold, Silver

Every step has its rhyme and reason. This step may take the longest to complete because not only will there be lag time between your advisor analyzing your data and presenting the recommendations, but this is also the time where you'll likely have the most questions. There may be some recommendations that you need further explanation on, or some that you outright disagree with and both are fine.

There shouldn't be any time within any of these steps that you don't feel free to voice your concerns, but especially at this point because everything has been laid out on the table and you know where you are and what your advisor believes will be the best route to pursue your goals. Sometimes, your objection to a recommendation may be a result of just not understanding, and you must voice that. There's a big danger in not voicing your questions and concerns. You don't want to move forward with a recommendation you're not fully comfortable with because you simply won't have peace behind it. You may worry day and night, even if it's the right choice. You may be inclined to say "no" simply because you don't understand and are too ashamed or afraid to admit to your confusion. If you don't speak up, you may end up saying "no" to what you need to say "yes" to.

No advisor should have to force you to make a decision, but you have to commit yourself to making a decision regardless of the answer. If you say you need to think about it, give yourself a time frame by which you will make a decision. Whether it's two days, three days, or a week, so be it. Don't put it off. Life doesn't stop, and a million things are constantly tugging at us, so we must do our best to prioritize items and make decisions while the information is fresh and still top of mind. As the days go by, it will become even more tempting to put it near the bottom of the pile and allow other things to take precedence. But consider all the things we often put ahead of making important decisions and how our prioritization often conflicts with the very things that could profit us in the end. I completely understand everyone has different ways of making a decision and the fear of making the wrong decision is always present, but putting things off and doing nothing could be the worst decision. There will never be a perfect time to do anything, so you might as well do it now. Now that we've done the hardest parts of picking a financial advisor, defining and establishing your goals, data gathering and analyzing and recommendations, we can now put our recommendations into action.

Step 5: Plan Implementation

The implementation process is typically the easiest and most fun part for both you and your advisor. Advisors get excited as they observe clients go from nervousness, anxiety, or uncertainty, to relief, excitement, and confidence concerning their financial future. Clients are obviously excited for the same reasons, but even more because their financial future is now moving into the direction it needs to go to pursue their goals.

The implementation process is also the easiest because it's usually a matter of just filling out paperwork. All the paperwork is prepared by your advisor. You just review for accuracy and sign.

Step 6: Monitor, Review & Adjust

You've made it the final step, but you can't take your hands off the wheel. Some of the unintended events that happen financially are a result of taking the Ron Propel stance to retirement: "set it and forget it." Nothing goes exactly as you planned, so staying on top of our ever-changing world is vital. Here are a few ways how:

Monthly & Quarterly Statements

This may not sound like something that would need explaining, but you would be surprised how many people don't read their statements on a regular basis, especially during volatile markets. Your statements not only tell you what's going on with your accounts, but are also your opportunity to identify any errors.

Periodic Reviews

Another aspect of your relationship with your advisors is periodic review of your assets. Over the years, I've noticed a pattern where people don't feel the need to meet as much in good markets and they want to meet more frequently during negative markets, and both are wrong. You should have regular reviews no matter what. There may be circumstances where you need to meet more than frequently, but reviews should occur with some form of normalcy.

The frequency of your reviews will depend on what type of investment you have, but could be quarterly, semi-annually, or at the bare minimum annually. Typically, as you begin a relationship with your advisor, you may desire to meet more frequently to become familiar with your documents or your advisor's process. Over time those meetings may become less frequent. Michigan, for example, has many "snowbirds" –people who fly south during the winter. In these cases, meetings may be conducted over the phone or video conference, but they happen regularly.

Adjustments

As we've seen up to this point, most of the items we've put into place have been based on several estimations and desires. We know everything won't go as planned, so you need to have some room for adjustments along the way. The staple to everything will always be the plan, but the plan will still need to be adjusted over time. Life changes, as do your goals and needs. Sometimes spouses, children, and parents become dependents, or pass during your retirement, and these circumstances could call for a change in income on your part. As we touched on earlier, retirees frequently get excited in the early years of their retirement and tend to overspend in the early years only to then have to adjust their income in later years to make their money last longer.

If you move, the amount you were paying in property taxes and homeowner's insurance is replaced by rent or homeowner's association dues. Care may be needed for you or a spouse which would require more income, regardless if it's a nursing home or in-home health care. You may at some point during retirement realize there's a chance you won't use all your assets and may start to think about estate and charitable giving. You may have a taxable estate and need to decide to either spend down assets or find a way to tax efficiently transfer them to your heirs.

I can't tell you what exactly will change during your life in retirement, but there will be changes, and the more details you have planned out in your retirement, the easier it will be to make those adjustments.

For Small Business Owners

The upside of being a small business owner is that you get to make all the decisions, but that's also the downside of being a small business owner. Many entrepreneurs must make decisions regarding their business and personal life, which intertwine daily. A lot of small business owners put off planning for retirement because they feel they don't have time to do it, but you can't afford to not do it. Entrepreneurs, please make sure you're working with a knowledgeable accountant, attorney and financial advisor. This may sound like a lot of money, but it's an investment into your well-being.

Far too many small business owners aren't prepared for retirement, and sometimes it's a matter of certain things being missed. You must force yourself to save for your retirement. Being in the right retirement plan is vital to you and your family's longevity. The wrong plan can affect not only the size of your nest egg, but also the income taxes you pay each year. You may end up paying unnecessary income taxes simply because you weren't aware of your options.

For instance, a basic IRA allows you to save $5,500-$6,500 (as of 2018) each year, but as a small business owner, depending on your structure and sales, this number could inflate to over $50,000. Again, depending on the type of business you own, not only could you set up your own 401K or 403B plan, even if it's just you and your spouse, but you also have the ability to create your own pension.

Many, if not most business owners have the majority of their wealth tied up in their business without a clear-cut plan on how they will get the money out of the business. According to a study done by a large financial institution, they found the average retirement age for business owners they surveyed was around 68, which tends to be later than most people who work for someone else.

Small business retirement planning is a specialized area of planning that must be taken seriously. Otherwise, you could wake up 65 years old with nothing saved.

15 Asset Protection

Now you've made it into the big leagues. You've started with the foundation of understanding the purpose of money and how to honor God financially. Once you laid that foundation, you began to take the first steps by working, planning, and budgeting. With the foundation of biblical wealth management, you started to see the fruit of your labor. You've saved, given, invested, and now it's time to protect that wealth. Protecting your assets is vital. If you don't take measures to protect what you have even as it is being built, you may not be able to continue with the plan you set for yourself. Asset protection primarily comes in the form of various insurance policies as well as proper estate planning. Some of these measures are taken at different times, but you'll apply them as you need moving forward. If you go back to the six areas of wealth management, risk management is the foundation to wealth management. Though we are somewhat going out of order for explanation purposes, you want to make sure you consistently go back to ensure the foundation is solid.

If I were to ask you what your number one asset is, what would your answer be? Your bank account, your 401K, your business, your home? All these things are important and if you have any or all of them, they are indeed assets you want to protect, but none of them are your number one asset –you are! That's right. Your ability to work and earn a living is your number one asset. So, what are you doing to protect it? Unless you inherited some of the things listed above, wasn't it you and your ability to work, save and invest that led to you obtaining these things? We've already discussed some of these items, but it's good to review them in this context as well.

Disability Insurance

Studies show that someone 40 or younger is much more likely to become disabled than die prematurely. If you're retired, disability insurance isn't necessary because you're likely drawing social security and/or a pension that will continue for the rest of your life under all circumstances. However, if you're still working you need to make sure you have disability insurance. For my retirees, don't mentally check out because I'm going to show you how to protect your other assets.

There are a few things you can do to protect your number one asset. The first thing relates to how we personally care for our bodies through proper diet, exercise, and rest. Some disabilities occur from the way we care for our bodies, so we must take care to prevent these things. Financially speaking, the number one way of protecting your income comes in the form of disability insurance.

People often get worker's compensation and disability insurance mixed up. To be clear, worker's comp is designed to protect employees if they are hurt on the job or contract an illness because of work conditions. Disability insurance is designed to replace your income in the instance you lose the ability to work due to injury or illness, regardless of where it happens.

You may have seen advertisements where a duck tells you that this company offers a service to "pay your bills" if you can't work. Though they offer various options, many times they are referring to disability insurance. Think of a surgeon who cuts him/herself while preparing dinner and permanently causes nerve damage to their hand and can no longer operate. Disability insurance would replace their income.

Just like any insurance contract, the definitions in your policy are what are most important in determining what you may or may not receive in a situation of disability. To be considered disabled and receive benefits from the social security administration, you must be unable to engage in any substantial gainful activity (SGA) by reason of any medically determinable physical or mental impairment(s) which can be expected to result in death or which has lasted or can be expected to last for a continuous period of not less than 12 months. For reasons that are apparent, it can be very difficult to receive disability benefits from Social Security, to the point where some must wait years and hire attorneys to receive benefits. So, imagine, if you get sick or hurt, do you want to put all your hopes in the requirements to qualify for Social Security?

Individual disability insurance policies are usually a bit less strict about the "definition" of disability. Disability Insurance policies will usually pay benefits after what they call an "elimination period" which is typically 30-90 days. This means that they won't pay for benefits for the first three months after you're deemed disabled.

The elimination period is an important component, but the most important is if your benefits will pay and for how long, and that is determined by whether your disability is determined by "own occupation" or "any occupation." Any occupation says that unless you're completely disabled, you won't receive benefits if you can work "any occupation." So, the surgeon from our previous paragraph can't perform surgery, but could work as a receptionist in a hospital. In this case, your benefits could likely be denied. This by no means suggests working as a receptionist in a hospital isn't honorable or important work because it is, but it doesn't consider your training and job experience, and therefore "own occupation" policies are vital for certain occupations

Own occupation says that if you're unable to work the job you're experienced in and trained to do, you can collect benefits, and in some cases, you may be able to work somewhere else because you can't perform your previous position. Own occupation considers your education, your experience, your most recent position, and your income, which is what disability insurance is set out to protect. As you can expect, own occupation policies are more expensive because of the very reason that if you do have to step away from work, you're not only more likely to be able to collect benefits, but your benefits may be higher than an "any occupation" policy.

Some policies will pay for a couple years depending on the cause of disability and the type of policy, while others will pay up to the Social Security age of either 62 or 65. Some policies will also pay benefits to replace some portion of your income if you must go from working full-time to part-time. Some will also make your student loan payments and make retirement type contributions on your behalf. The cost of your policy will depend on several factors, such as if it's an individually owned policy or a group policy through work. Just like with any insurance, whether it's health, life or disability insurance, the group policy is almost always going to be less expensive than buying the policy on your own. Not only do you have a group rate because of the number of people in the plan, but it's also going to be cheaper because you typically can't take the policy with you if you leave the company.

An individually owned policy allows you to customize the policy to your needs, but your cost will depend on several things such as your age, overall health, income and occupation. If you are a police officer, firefighter, a pilot, or any other profession that would include an increased risk of being injured, you may find your policy more expensive or difficult to purchase. Jobs that are not viewed as dangerous, but maybe prone to higher levels of stress may also increase your overall costs.

Another feature that comes with disability policies but may also increase the cost is a guaranteed renewability feature which states that once your policy is issued, as long as you make your premium they must continue your coverage. The insurance company can increase your premium if they increase the cost for everyone within the same risk class. For example, if you're a lawyer, they may consider your risk (A) class. If they increase your premium it also means they increased the costs for all other "A Class" lawyers.

Another feature that will increase the cost of your disability policy is if it's issued with an inflation or future increase provision. Inflation riders allow the benefits to grow to combat cost of living increases. Future increase allows you to increase your coverage while you're working as your career advances and your income grows.

Assume you're a lawyer who makes $75,000 right out of college, but 10 years into your field you make partner and now you're making $350,000. At this point in time a $75,000 disability policy doesn't do you as good because you'd only be covered for about 21% of your current income. The future increase rider allows you to increase your coverage as your income increases, but of course with more coverage comes more cost.

One of the final things that will affect the cost of your policy is how much of your income would be replaced in the event you become disabled. You may think this is silly to even think about because we would want all our income to be replaced. The reality is insurance companies will typically only cover a maximum of 60-70% of your income. Why? Because the insurance policy's goal is to replace your after-tax income. Disability Insurance policies cannot replace the portion of your income that was paid in taxes.

You should also know that benefits received under a disability policy *should* be income tax free. I emphasize the word "should" because if you select disability coverage through your employer you'll likely see two options after you select your coverage: "employer paid" and "employee paid." The definitions are straight forward, but what isn't so clear is the outcome if you became disabled and collected benefits under these provisions.

In a group plan, if you decide to pay for the coverage, that means any benefits received would be income tax free to you on the other end because you're paying your insurance premiums out of your after-tax income. If you elect for your employer to pay the premium for you, benefits would be taxed, which would not be the ideal situation considering you're already receiving less than your full amount of income.

Disability insurance isn't really talked about much, so you must sit down and decide what the most logical choice for your situation is. Many people find themselves in situations where they may not be able to afford an individual policy and must go with the group, which is fine. It's better than having nothing and the difference in costs could be drastic. A group rate may be $30 a month, where an individual rate could be $200 per month. Your situation may call for you to have both group and individual policies.

Disability Insurance for Small Business Owners

Small business owners must approach purchasing disability insurance with more focus and rigor than most people because, often, you are the business and it likely can't run without you, so what happens if you as a small business owner become disabled and you can't work? What happens to your income and your family? What about your business and any possible employees, as well as their families if suddenly you can't work? As a small business owner, everything is riding on your ability to work much more than people who work for a business they don't own or run.

Disability insurance for small business owners can take the form of two different policies. One is an individual policy for you, and the other one is a business overhead insurance policy. Your individual policy is very similar to your neighbor who works for a national corporation, where the policy separates your personal income from the overall business expenses and operational costs. If your business shows a gross of $20,000 per month, and your personal income is $10,000 per month, your personal disability policy would cover your portion, the $10,000. Business overhead insurance essentially infuses cash into your business to cover the costs of running the business to keep it going. In our example where the business makes $20,000 a month, let's assume it costs $5,000 per month to cover the monthly costs for the business to run. A business overhead policy would infuse the business with the $5,000 per month in the event you become disabled.

It's important to note two things with business overhead insurance. For one, it only covers the business's true "overhead costs" and not your income or salary. Second, most insurance companies will limit how long they will pay out for the policy (i.e. two years.) They limit how long they'll pay because they assume if you haven't returned to work within that time frame it's unlikely you will be able to return, which makes estate planning very important for everyone, but especially for a small business owner. (We'll discuss Estate Planning in more detail later.)

Liability/Umbrella Policy

Umbrella policies are much like disability policies in the sense that it's something that most people should have but are unaware that it exists and why it exists. An umbrella policy stands in place to cover you and your assets if you're found liable for damages that might be paid in various situations. Umbrella policies will typically pay benefits after another policy you own has exhausted their limits. Umbrella policies could cover you not only in personal dealings but also business dealings.

Imagine you're driving your car and not paying attention and rear end someone causing personal damages to the driver of the other car in the amount of $300,000. What do you do if your auto policy only covers $200,000? What about if someone has a slip and fall on your porch that you didn't feel like shoveling and breaks their leg causing $350,000 in damages, and your homeowner's policy only covers $250,000? If you own a business or rental property and you're found liable for more than what your policy will pay, you must have a way of coming up with the rest of the money. This could mean selling valuable investments, cleaning out bank accounts, or even selling homes and businesses. Situations like this happen more frequently than you probably expect.

I've actually known people who have business or rental properties and scoff at the idea of an umbrella policy because their business is an "LLC" and in a liability situation only their businesses' assets would be at risk. But why risk giving up those when you could purchase a liability policy in some cases for a couple hundred dollars per year? A couple hundred dollars could be the only thing separating you from better protecting your assets. To make things even simpler, most insurance companies that issue homeowner's policies can attach it to your homeowner's policy.

Another interesting caveat to an umbrella policy is that most of them will pay for you to hire a lawyer and trial costs if you're accused of things like slander, libel, and other infractions.

Time to talk to your local home and auto insurance agent.

Long-Term Care Insurance

One of the essential elements of retirement planning (which we covered earlier) is determining expenses in retirement. Undoubtedly the hardest expenses to predict are medical costs. Medical costs tend to be the most concerning area for both soon-to-be retirees and already retirees. It's an area that continues to increase at much higher rates than the cost of living and ends up being some retirees' largest cost outside of housing. Coincidentally, the unpredictability of medical costs results in many retirees underestimating their income needs.

According to long-termcare.gov, long-term care is described as "is a range of services and supports you may need to meet your *personal care* needs." Most long-term care is not medical care, but rather assistance with the basic activities of daily living (ADL). Statistics suggest the possibility of you requiring this type of care is much more common than you might think. The Department of Human and Health Services suggests people who're currently 65 years of age have a 70% chance of needing this type of care, which is seldom a desired outcome, but may at times be necessary. My mother-in-law looked after her father for a few months when he could no longer care for himself, and even as a registered nurse, she realized she couldn't give him the care he needed and had to put him in a nursing home. The transition to a nursing home can be very difficult for both the person going to the nursing home, and the relative who may have to decide to put them in, but the most painful part may be the cost associated with this type of care.

One big misconception is Medicare will pay for nursing home care permanently. Medicare may cover up to 100 days of a nursing home stay that is preceded by a hospital stay. If you recognize that mom or dad is getting to the point where they can't handle care for themselves and decide on Saturday to put them in an assisted living facility on Monday, this stay won't be covered under Medicare. You also need to keep in mind that Medicaid is for low-income individuals, so if you have any sort of assets you most likely won't qualify. Even if you do qualify you have limited to no control over where you or your loved one goes, nor do you have any say in possible roommates.

Medical costs and nursing home care expenses have become very devastating for some retirees because the money they assumed would be available for income is going towards medical costs. This also becomes troublesome for married couples and those who have dependent children. I've seen several times where a spouse had to go into a nursing home and depleted assets that were allocated as income to last for both retirees' lives. There are a few things that can be done to try and curb this expense, but for simplicity purposes we'll focus on long-term care insurance.

Long-term care insurance is specifically designed to either lower or eliminate the burden of the expenses for long-term illness and impairments. This should not be confused with long-term disability insurance which is for loss of income from employment due to sickness or injury. LTC has become a "hot topic" over the past few years because both clients and advisors acknowledge the danger of avoiding the conversation. Similar to the life insurance conversation, some people tend to feel if they don't have the conversation about long-term care insurance they won't ever need it. Avoiding the conversation won't eliminate the need for LTC insurance, but properly planning for possible needs could be the very "thing" that saves your retirement, your spouse's retirement if applicable, and your heir's inheritance.

Like any insurance, traditional long-term care does pose the risk of paying premiums for years and then never using the insurance, but there's always the risk of finding yourself in a position where you need it and don't have it. LTC insurance can get very expensive because of the nature of the policy; it's used to provide payment for what could be expensive care. LTC insurance will likely increase in cost, especially if you purchase a policy with an inflation rider. Inflation riders can be just as important as owning a policy, especially if you purchase the policy years before you need the care it provides.

With the big cloud of uncertainty surrounding LTC policies, some people outright reject them. As a matter of fact, several companies over the last few years have exited the long-term business. I can only speculate as to why, but I think the companies are just as concerned about the uncertainty as customers.

These various conundrums have led many companies to offer alternatives to approaching possible long-term care needs. Some annuities offer increased income if LTC services are required. Others offer a hybrid product that provides income for long-term care needs, and a death benefit if the long term care need never takes place. Either way, I think you can see just like any other things in life, nothing is risk free, and the biggest mistake is not realizing the risk is present, or while acknowledging the presence of risk, deciding not to act to eliminate or reduce the risk.

16 Estate Planning

Essentially, all financial planning can be boiled down to these six different, yet intertwined areas: Financial Position, Insurance, Investments, Retirement Planning, Taxes and Estate Planning. Much like life insurance, estate planning is one of those where people push to the back burner.

As you read through this section, you may recall some personal scenarios that could have and should have been avoided if someone took up the mantle of taking care of estate planning. The estate planning process can be time consuming and take a lot of thought and energy, but as my estate attorney told me, "I'm either going to get my money now (upfront) or later (when you die), but if I get it later, it's going to cost you more."

There's always going to be a cost associated with anything, so the reason behind not doing an estate plan should not be to save money. Attorneys typically charge by the hour, and if one of your heirs must hire them after you pass away, they'll likely have to pay a lot more. This common misunderstanding suggests that there's no need for estate planning if you don't have a large estate, which isn't true. Without a proper estate plan, your heirs may not even know where to go and how to receive the items you left for them. Estate planning is a general term and the exact items that should be included in your estate plan may differ from mine, but you should have something in place that lists your possessions as well as your wishes, instructions, and the beneficiaries of your estate in the event of your passing.

Another big misconception about estate planning is it's only to take care of things after you die, and that's not true. It also includes the time when you're alive but unable to take care of your affairs as in the case of disability, incapacitation, or your unwillingness to take care of business. The main goal of estate planning is to manage and transfer assets in the timeliest fashion while paying the least amount of taxes possible.

Much of completing an estate plan has to do with looking long-term. As you think about the people who will manage your assets, think about these three words: trust, time, knowledge. Choose someone whom you trust, who will have the time to commit to doing the job properly, and who has knowledge about your wishes and overall wealth management.

No matter who you choose, please make sure you work with an experienced estate attorney. Some estate planning documents don't require an attorney, some do. You want to make sure you're dealing with the person who specializes in this area. Think from a medical standpoint. You wouldn't go to the foot doctor for heart surgery, nor should you go to a trial attorney for your estate planning needs unless they are an estate attorney. A basic, estate plan typically consists of five documents:

1. Medical Power of Attorney
2. HIPPA Agent
3. Power of Attorney
4. Will
5. Trusts

Medical Power of Attorney

Your medical power of attorney would step in in the instance where you can't make decisions for yourself. Your medical power of attorney is an individual or individuals to whom you give the responsibility of making medical decisions on your behalf. Consider someone being in a car accident and unable to respond, the medical POA can make decisions regarding care. Like any POA, most of them require that multiple medical professionals attest to the fact that you need assistance to make these decisions, but you have to make sure whoever you name is very clear about your medical history and your wishes. Decisions such as whether you want to be kept alive by medical equipment are included. You want to make sure you record your wishes concerning your care because your loved ones should know what you want, while keeping in mind that you have given them authorization to make this choice. What's right is not always apparent or easy.

I recall the story of the father of someone close to me who'd lost consciousness and contracted an illness where he had to be on a ventilator. Doctors told them their father wouldn't recover and if he did he would live his life as a vegetable. They also said he wouldn't have a quality of life and to let him go. Through prayer, the family decided not to do it and over a decade later dad is still here. He still has some health challenges, but he's content with the fact that God spared his life. This is a prime example of why your plans, wishes, and decision makers should be well documented.

Some decisions may be a matter of life and death, and others could turn into life or death scenarios if not handled properly. Some of the things your medical POA may need to decide on is if and what medications you should receive, as well as what examinations, procedures, surgeries and treatment plans should take place. If possible, it's likely in your best interests for this person to be the same as your HIPAA agent.

HIPAA Agent

Some states call it a patient advocate, and some will call this a HIPAA agent, but this is the person/s to whom you give authority to release and discuss your medical records. This is a document that some people believe they'll never need, but there are very good reasons why you want this in place. For one, it's a federal law that provides privacy protection concerning your medical history.

When it comes to accessing medical records and determining who can access them, the HIPAA agent should be in place because many hospitals and doctors' offices will limit what's allowed to be released. Your HIPAA agent can access your medical records prior to incapacitation and can also be present during the discussion of your medical treatment. Without this document in hand, medical facilities will not authorize the release of medical information to a third party, nor will they allow your information to be shared. While these laws are for your protection, this can clearly be a problem if you're injured and your loved one needs to consult with medical professionals, or just wants to get more understanding about a certain aspect of your medical history. Even if it's your spouse, there are limits on what information can be shared without this document. This can be problematic for friends or relatives to seek counsel on your behalf if they don't have information regarding your medical history.

Much like everyone else on this estate planning list, the person you name as your patient advocate needs to be someone you can trust and who has the ability to make these decisions. The emphasis here is on ability and not trust. I don't think you would name someone whom you didn't trust to access your medical records, but there are people you might trust who might not have the ability to take care of you. Someone who struggles under pressure or who is very indecisive is probably not the person you want in this situation because of the severity of the circumstances. You also want to make sure whomever you choose knows your desires and shares the same value system as you do.

Power of Attorney

What most people call a regular power or attorney is the person/s to whom you're giving the authorization to manage your non-medical affairs. Just like the other power of attorneys, this POA steps into the scenario if you're unwilling or unable to handle your affairs pertaining to your property and possessions. These items can include preparing and filing tax returns, renting, buying, or selling real estate, trading stocks, paying bills, and essentially everything else that you would normally do yourself. This POA tends to be the one most people are familiar with.

As with any other legal document, you want to give careful consideration to whom you give this authorization because, depending on how you set this up, this person may have just as much authority as you would have over your own possessions. Having a POA can save you a lot of hassle in the end if assistance is needed. Without a POA on file, if you go into the hospital for a short or extended period of time, something as simple as getting a bill paid, cashing a check on your behalf, or checking on overdraft fees that were a result of an account having no overseer can become problematic. Banks will turn your family member or friend away without a power of attorney on file.

Having a POA is all about being proactive and setting things up ahead of time. That way, if and when it's needed, there isn't a delay in what could be a critical moment.

Many of you are likely thinking, "I don't want anyone having that type of access to my funds." To address that concern, let's review the different types of power of attorney.

1. **Durable**

    Your durable power of attorney is the broadest of them all because this is essentially giving another person/s authorization to transact business as you would at any time. While you still have all your faculties, you can revoke the POA privileges from the person you name, but once the durable POA is filed and you were to become incapacitated, revoking the POA would usually come as a result of someone abusing their rights which would have to be proven in a court which would require an attorney and, of course, money to follow. While some of the other POA roles have either limits or requirements before someone can transact business on your behalf, durable power of attorney has no such prerequisites.

In the instance with my wife and I, we both have durable POA for each other out of convenience more than anything. If there were a situation where we had to get something done and I was out of town, she could sign for me, or in the instance where I needed to transact business at our local bank and my wife simply didn't want to go to the bank, I could just sign the form for her and it would be as official as if she did it herself. Obviously, this type of POA requires the utmost trust in a person, but as I said before, you also need to make sure whomever you name has the ability and time to make decisions on your behalf. A durable POA also helps in the instance that if something were to happen at a later date where either one of us couldn't handle our affairs, we have provisions within the document to limit other people's access or fulfill requirements before they would be able to transact business on our behalf.

2. **Limited POA**

As is the case with all power of attorney designations, the limits to a "limited" POA will be based on the relationship between you and your appointed agent, and the scope of business you desire them to manage for you. The limits could hypothetically be transactions where you only allow your real estate agent to transact real estate business, or one of your children can only transact banking business or bill pay on your behalf. The limits also typically relate to time, where you give someone either full or limited access for a limited amount of time.

Let's stay with the example that you work with a real estate agent you completely trust in the manner of handling real estate transactions. You need to close a business deal concerning real estate, but you must be out of town, or you are physically having problems and can't travel to the local loan closing. With a limited POA, you could essentially give your agent a limited POA for the day you anticipate closing your real estate deal, or within a few days. Assume you and your seller agree to close your real estate deal on July 15, but you know from past dealings things don't always go as anticipated, so you assign your real estate agent to only transact real estate business on your behalf from July 15th to July 20th. You can also include more protective guards where you allow them to transact only purchases or sales, up to a specific dollar amount.

A limited power of attorney can be used for many special situations and it may not ever come up in your life, but it's good to know that it's there if you need it. You'd be surprised how many people take advantage of things like this once they learn how it works.

3. *Springing POA*

Springing power of attorney could be either durable, where your agent has the authorization to act as you in all situations, or limited in transaction, time, or a combination of the two. What makes springing POAs different is they typically aren't enforceable until an event happens, or, as the name says, they "spring" into action after certain stipulations are met.

Many times, springing POA forms are used in relation to a medical condition. Often, the hardest part of estate planning is not expressing your wishes, but determining who will manage your affairs for you. For those who fear someone may take advantage of them, or just don't want to relinquish control of their assets, they may require the affirmation of two medical professionals that you can't manage your affairs and need assistance.

Power of attorney forms come in many shapes and sizes, and it's important that you work with a knowledgeable estate attorney to make sure you do the correct thing for your situation. It's important that you do a full estate plan and not just power of attorneys because those POAs become null and void once you die. If you name a power of attorney, and lack the rest of these other documents, your heirs may find themselves in probate court.

Will

At its basic stripped-down purpose, a will is essentially your written instructions regarding the distribution of your tangible assets. Simply put, it's your letter to a judge. Within your will, you will typically list your assets and your giving instructions as to who gets what upon your death. Many times the list includes property such as clothes, cars, homes, jewelry, antiques, and businesses. Some people put stickers on the bottom of items to indicate who gets them, but it's important that your instructions are clear.

When you're dealing with financial assets, it's important to note that places like banks, insurance companies, retirement plans, etc., typically won't acknowledge the instructions of a will if those institutions have beneficiaries listed on their documents. Financial institutions typically function under contract law, which means they will go by whatever instructions you name on their documents.

For instance, if you have a life insurance policy that you wanted to leave to your spouse, but on your beneficiary form with the life insurance company you name your sister, the life insurance company is typically going to pay the proceeds to your sister. Same goes for bank and retirement accounts. I use the word "typically" because there are always exceptions to the rule, but in instances where that didn't happen, lawyers were involved which means less money to whomever received the proceeds.

Speaking of lawyers, one of the biggest misconceptions regarding wills is they don't have to go through probate court, and the truth is the complete opposite. Even though it's your instructions, wills must go through probate court and there are times where people must hire estate attorneys to help settle the affairs, which would typically result in your heirs getting less funds, or no funds at all. Bickering with relatives can cause the settling of an estate to drag out and a large chunk of a family's would-be inheritance gets gobbled up in fees.

Another downside of having only a will is the fact that your information becomes public record once it goes into probate court. Not only can people know how much you were worth, but also who your beneficiaries are and how much they will receive. This could be troublesome if you or your heirs owe someone. In this situation, someone could contest your estate and drag things out in court with your family.

The sad thing about contested estates is that some of the allegations aren't even legit. There are times where a family is looking to receive funds from an estate, and somehow, some relative pops up out of nowhere whom you might not know or haven't seen in 20 years, and now things are back in court. This may not always be the case. There are times where because of the size of the estate, or because spouses, siblings, and children have an agreement and avoid the fights, things go smoothly, but we all know money tends to bring out the worst in people and I would err on the side of caution.

The will is just one piece of estate planning and, while you don't want to have it as your only document, it's better than not having it at all. A more recent, high-profile example of this is the musician "Prince." He died without a will and left an estate estimated anywhere from $300-$500 million. When that happens, not only is there often a family dispute, but you leave the courts to decide how your assets are to be divided, which may not be what you desire. Not only that, but if you don't have a will that names a personal representative or executor, the court may elect someone to be your personal representative of your will that you would not desire to handle your affairs.

Another portion of your will is assigning a guardian for your children to name who would take them in and care for them as you would. Sometimes this is your parents, siblings, their godparents, or whomever you choose to raise your little ones. This would also be important if you have a special needs child or aging parent.

Another aspect of not having a will is if assets are left to a minor, they have uncapped access to the funds at certain ages. In the state of Michigan, this age is 18. Can you imagine an 18-year-old getting their hands on $250,000? I've seen it several times, and we call it in the financial services business a good year, because the assets often don't last beyond a year.

A will is one of the few estate planning documents that doesn't have to be created with an attorney, which is why you see some services that offer you pretty much a fill in the blank program. As long as the will is witnessed *and notarized*, it's legally binding. I would suggest working with an estate attorney to draft your will. But keep in mind, wills often work best when accompanied with a trust.

Trusts

The trust is one of the most powerful, yet underutilized tools available. A trust is typically the best way to avoid probate and retain control over the assets from beyond the grave. Some don't use it because, I suspect, they know very little about it, or they believe they don't need it.

"Trust fund" kids in real life and the movies are often portrayed as rich, and people mistakenly believe that trusts are only for what we would consider wealthy or rich. That's just not the case. Estate planning is just as much about having order as it is protection, and we must remember that we do serve a God of purpose and order and we need to do the same. Trusts are like wills in that you're giving instructions, but there are some important differences between trusts and wills.

For one, unlike wills, trusts must be created by an attorney. When choosing an attorney, keep in mind that the law is very broad and though some attorneys may offer to do an estate plan for you, you want to seek out an estate attorney who specializes in the services you need. Again, you wouldn't go to a foot specialist to care for a heart condition. Another major difference, and some may tell you it's the biggest difference, is the fact that trusts are private manners, meaning they don't typically have to go through probate court. When your assets are in a trust, they can quickly flow from the trusts to your heirs without disputes in court.

Another key benefit of a trust is you can include specific instructions as to who will get the assets and what conditions must be met for assets to be received. The interesting thing is you can be as creative as you want regarding the stipulations, especially in the instance where you either are dealing with minors, adult children with special needs, or relatives who make unwise financial decisions. You can even include stipulations such as the trust would pay for a maximum of five years of college for your kids, but only if they maintained a particular grade point average. In the case of minors, many trusts stipulate they won't have access to the money or at least a large sum of it until they reach a certain age like 25 or 30. Until they hit that age, the person in charge (trustee) can pay for any of their needs including health, education, maintenance and support. Your children's needs will be met.

Also, funds held in a trust are protected from creditors so long as the assets remain in the trust. If funds are held in a trust for the benefit of someone else, those creditors can't get to those funds as long as they are still in the trust. The beneficiary may have the option to remove the funds at certain ages, but they aren't required to. These stipulations often help prevent heirs from making unwise financial decisions either because of age or history. If you have a relative who has a history of making bad decisions. Chances are, a windfall of money won't change that, but may actually make the situation worse.

Another aspect of creating a trust is not only thinking about who gets what and under what conditions, but who will manage the affairs on your behalf if you are unable or unwilling. Within the trust, trustees are the acting parties, and typically while you're alive or still coherent, you and your spouse (if applicable) operate as the trustees. Upon your death or incapacitation, your trustees would step in and handle your affairs just as you would, similar to a power of attorney. The big difference is that the trustees still operate after your death, whereas the power of attorney becomes void at death.

As with all these legal documents, it's vital you name someone who's knowledgeable, trustworthy, and has the time to manage your affairs. It doesn't have to be a family member or friend. Some people name third parties who are unrelated to their family, such as a bank or lawyer to manage their affairs for them. If you name multiple trustees, you can also include safeguards that may require both to agree on anything concerning the trust's affairs. The sky is really the limit within your trust.

So, who may benefit from having a trust arrangement in place? Those who have a small business, who have done well financially, as well as those who have small children, or adult children and/or parents and relatives who rely on them. Imagine a young couple with children who leaves the kids with their parents for a vacation and tragically an accident happens and both parents die. The family must figure out who will take care of the kids. Now imagine that both parents had life insurance and bank accounts but only named each other as the beneficiary, or they named their minor children as beneficiaries. Since a minor can't handle the affairs, these assets would typically have to go through probate court where the courts will assign them a conservator who will handle the affairs for them. This process can be nothing less than cumbersome where the conservator must petition the court anytime they need to withdraw the funds for the children. But the biggest issue is not only does the court restrict what you can use the money for, but they also limit how you can save and/invest on their behalf.

Now, let's assume that this couple, instead, created an estate plan where they name their parents as not only conservators to handle the financial affairs, but also as guardians to physically care for the kids, and as successor trustees of the trust they created. Upon their death, their assets would be put into trust accounts for their kids, and the grandparents could now easily manage affairs for their grandkids without the court deciding how their grandkids receive their inheritance.

People who have special needs children should also consider a "special needs" trust which is specifically designed to protect assets for those who are most vulnerable.

There are also multiple types of trusts ranging from the simple to complex. Your simplest type of trust is typically going to be a revocable trust where you, as the trust creator, can "revoke" and make changes while you're alive, but once you die, the trust then becomes irrevocable and changes can't be made.

Most of our conversation has focused on personal assets, but it's quite common to see real estate and business assets placed in a trust for the same reason. To keep those interests out of court and in the hands of people whom you feel will properly handle things based on your desires. There are also irrevocable trusts while you are living. These are typically part of estate planning where someone desires to lower the value of their estate for estate tax purposes and will take assets and place them in a trust where the trust owner/grantor can no longer access them, and these assets are set aside for either their heirs, a charity, or used specifically for estate tax purposes.

Trusts can be as boring or as fun as you would like them to be, but what you pay is worth it in the end for you and your family. Costs vary, and estate planning is not cheap. But when you compare it against the cost of some of the other things that command our dollars each year, this option yields more fruit in the long run. If you lack an estate plan, you could essentially be ruining the opportunity to leave an inheritance for your children and grandchildren. Remember what my own estate attorney said, "I'm going to get my money either way. But if I get it up front, it's going to cost you a lot less than if I get it on the back end."

17   Wealth Killers

Before I conclude, I want to address a few "Wealth Killers." Wealth killers are financial decisions some of us have likely made at some point in our lives and may still be making right now. These are often very subtle behaviors and ideas that are contrary to what Scripture teaches and are the very things that are killing the church financially.

Identifying and uprooting these financial weeds helps us recognize and get rid of them if they sprout back up. These aren't things that happen overnight, and, just like medical conditions, spotting the symptoms of these wealth killers early on is going to be the key.

Living Off Credit

Job losses, illnesses and emergencies can cause people to turn to things like credit cards, home equity loans, and other lines of credit, but these certainly cannot account for every case. Living off credit, in many cases, is a by-product of not mastering the section of budgeting, saving and planning. We can't get ahead financially when we constantly owe someone. When you owe a creditor, your money is spent even before your money hits your hand.

Proverbs 22:7 states, *The rich rule over the poor and the borrower is slave to the lender.* This passage clearly explains the danger of debt and its bondage. When you're in bondage, you're restricted as to what you can do and how you do it, and this is the truth financially. Have there been times where you wanted to give to a charity, a relative in need or even a homeless person, but just didn't have the money to do it? These are the side effects of debt. If you're in deep constant debt you become a slave to whomever you owe. You're a slave, not financially free. Financially free does not necessarily mean wealthy, but if you can eliminate or prevent debt in your life, you have the freedom that some making higher incomes don't have. Modern day slaves aren't in chains, they're in debt. I don't want to confuse leveraging borrowing for business purposes, with living off credit. There are many times where burrowing for business purposes is not only easier, but is the best financial decision for you. This is not the scenario I'm referring to, but rather the situation where we can't survive without swiping a credit card.

Ignoring the Warning Signs

Everything that we think is an emergency really isn't, but it may be a result of ignoring warning signs. Sudden events do happen that have thrown our world into a whirlwind, but many times it's just the inevitable result of financial blind spots. How many of us have seen the car on "E," heard the bell ding and even see a message on our dashboard that says, "Fuel Level is Low," yet we continue to drive? What happens? You either barely make it to the next gas station, or you run out of gas.

Why do we allow these things to happen? We often act as though we have no control over our circumstances, while in most cases we do. When you know you're going to be on the road a lot and the gas gauge is close to the E, you fill up before you get going. Yet many of us ignore the warning signs and press our luck. Ignore the check engine light long enough and you could irreparably damage your car.

We all have those areas in our lives where there are warning signs. Financially, they could be overdrawing a bank account, having to remove money from a savings account each month, or borrowing from a 401(K). Proverbs 12:9 says, *The prudent see danger and take refuge, but the simple keep going and pay the penalty.* Even if you find yourself in a situation that isn't ideal, you must be able to see where your mistakes are and take refuge. That refuge could be in the form of debt counseling, an accountability partner, a budget, or paying a financial advisor to help you.

Too often we give ourselves too much credit and say things like, "I'll do better next time," but without a plan and accountability, nothing changes, and we continue to pay the penalty. That penalty may be debt stress, being a slave to the lender, a delayed or even an uneventful retirement, bankruptcy and the effect that it has on your credit.

Many people who approach retirement unprepared, knew it all along. They knew they should've been saving for retirement. They knew they should've been investing. They knew retirement would come, but they weren't ready. Again, I know misfortunes and tragedies do happen in people's lives, but many bankruptcies could've been avoided by simply grasping the foundation of this book.

It's never too late to change your path. It all starts with recognizing the financial dangers in your life.

Lifestyle Inflation

You may not be familiar with the concept of lifestyle inflation. It comes in two closely related phases. One, as your income increases over time, so does your lifestyle. For instance, you may decide to rent when you make $35,000, but later decide to purchase a home when you earn $100,000. Many people buy more expensive things when they receive a promotion or achieve a desired level of income as some sort of reward for their hard work.

Recall one of the foundations to biblically creating wealth is living below your means. Lifestyle inflation is dangerous because we often don't notice it. We know general inflation causes the cost of living to become more expensive, but if we aren't paying attention you may find yourself unable to save and invest money even though your income has increased over the years.

The second part of lifestyle inflation has to do with an old phrase:

"Keeping up with the Joneses." The "Joneses" in your world could be a neighbor, co-worker, sibling, friend or even your spouse. It's a senseless battle to see who can accumulate the most possessions. Many of us tend to be very competitive though we may not want each other to know it.

The main issue with keeping up with the Joneses is the covetous spirit that often drives the desire to not only keep up with the people, but eventually move past them. This is dangerous because, from the outside looking in, you have no idea what's going on with other people's finances. They could earn a higher income, which allows them certain things. They could have inherited something from a relative. Some people have also been more diligent and faithful with their finances, which may have allotted them the opportunity to have something we may desire; or they could just be faking. With the advancements in social media, we have the ability to paint a certain picture to the public, even if it's not reality. Though we often see it in children, we as adults often give in to peer pressure financially because we give in to the thought that success has a certain look. I talked with a former colleague, who bought suits from a very expensive clothier, although his salary didn't justify his purchases. The biggest issue with trying to keep up with the folks around us is that we end up indirectly saying to God that we don't appreciate what He has given us and is doing in our lives.

We all want to win, but there are times where the best way to win a battle is to not enter in the first place. Keeping up with the Joneses is a battle you don't want to enter. As long as your financial resources are focused on accumulating the most possessions, you will never be able to accumulate wealth and, in reality, you're ransoming your family's future.

This mentality starts as early as infancy where, as children we saw a child with a toy that we wanted, or we wanted the biggest and best toy compared to another child. Fast forward to elementary school, middle, and high school and getting the best toy mentality is exchanged for the best sneakers, designer jeans, or leather jackets. Fast forward beyond school and now we must get a nicer home, car, iPhone, electronics. Don't allow children, family, or society to pressure you into making bad financial decisions.

You can see the pattern and how it leads to financial ruins that often lasts generations. Proverbs 12:9 is one of the most important warnings in the Bible: "Better to be lowly and have a servant than to play the great man and lack bread." This verse deals directly with wisdom and pride which is the root of much of the "keeping up with Joneses" mentality. This can take the form of a lack of humility, a need for affirmation, or a combination of the two.

I've yet to meet an affluent person who wants you to know what's in their bank account. Most of them were very unassuming, humble and were the epitome of "lowly and had a servant." Maybe not a servant in the sense of someone waiting on them hand and foot, but from the stance that they could afford practically anything they wanted. This tends to be the exception and not the rule. Unfortunately, we see more people who buy things and go places they can't afford just to try and fit in with a crowd or just look important. This is a worldly view of what success is and is a sign that we have given in to societal pressures. Society says you need to have a degree, make a certain amount of money, live in this neighborhood, have gone to this country, drive this car, wear this designer, etc.

Many people, both within our society and within the church, haven't gotten a hold of biblical success and, despite their prestige and income, are failing. Biblical success, as it relates to our money, is the person who is diligent in their work and honors God financially through giving and wisdom. Biblical success is also the person who saves and can leave an inheritance for their children's children. Biblical success comes over time with wise decisions, not falling into get-rich-quick schemes.

If we look back to Proverbs 12:9, the lowly person as described in the Scripture could refer to someone who maybe doesn't have a public platform or name. Yet, this person still has a servant versus the person who is a show-off but lacks what they need. If we view this in common day terminology, it's the person who may wear expensive clothes or drive a nice car, yet they really don't have any money. Someone may not have the biggest house or wear name brand clothes, but they have put their children through school and still are able to save for retirement.

The only true measure of success is our obedience to God's calling on our lives. If you find yourself in a situation where you may not be making a lot of money but know you're in the space God has called you to be, you're successful, so keep holding on and moving forward.

Not Understanding Taxes

This is another place where the conversation may get a bit uncomfortable. Taxes come in a few different ways, but the most common are income taxes and property taxes.

In Mark 12, the Pharisees intentionally try to trap Jesus by asking him if it was right to pay the temple tax. The Jews were to be devoted to God in all they did, so paying the tax may be viewed as an allegiance to Rome. However, not paying the temple tax would be a direct violation to the law and viewed as a direct challenge of Caesar's authority. Jesus knew their intention and he also knew how both the Jews and the Roman government would respond to his answer, so what did he do? He simply took a coin, confirmed whose picture was on the coin (Caesar's) and said, "give to Caesar what is Caesar's and give to God what belongs to God."

Taxes are the law of the land, and not paying them only makes our lives a mess. For one, not paying the bill because we disagree with it doesn't make the bill go away. The bill doesn't go anywhere until it's paid. The longer you go without paying it, the larger it gets because of penalties and late charges. If the problems aren't dealt with a tax lien could be filed, which is a public record. This may prevent you from getting employment and your income or savings could be taken right out of your bank account. It's just an overall stressful situation that you don't want to find yourself in.

There are a few practical ways to avoid or eliminate this type of stress. For one, you must know who you are financially. Many times, these tax problems come from people who are self-employed or people who receive a lump sum of money from taxable sources like investments, business ventures, or retirement plans. You must understand your unique financial position and the best way to do that is to work with an accountant. Make sure you work with a certified professional. An accountant will be able to tell you what you can and can't do as far as lowering your tax burden, and put plans in place to keep you out of trouble.

Many times, we add stress to our lives by constantly living in a state of fear from simply not knowing something. Avoiding dealing with taxes because we're afraid of what may happen is like avoiding the doctor because you may think you'll get a bad report. Many times, things aren't nearly as bad as we think they are if we confront them early in the process.

The key is to understand how taxes work, and how you can minimize your taxes both now and later. Minimizing taxes now may come in the form of financial organization. Many allowable deductions on your taxes may get lost if you're not keeping track of them. If you own a business or real estate, there are many write-offs and deductions available to lower your taxes. From an investment standpoint, this is where investing in vehicles like municipal bonds, life insurance, ROTH IRA's, and regular brokerage accounts can save you taxes now, and in the future when you utilize the money. Appropriate estate planning can also help mitigate both income taxes, and estate taxes. Though taxes are a normal part of our lives, they also can play a big role in the erosion of wealth if you're not conscious of the tax system and how it works. This is another area where having wise counsel will serve you well.

Insufficient Life Insurance

We've already gone through the planning part of our conversation in addition to the life insurance section, but it is vital that you grasp the concept of owning the correct amount of life insurance. Some life insurance is better than no life insurance, but not having enough coverage or having the incorrect type of policy can still put your family and community in a financial bind.

Many people are financially struggling and living paycheck to paycheck. It's often hard to look ahead. But can you imagine how different families, communities, and the body of Christ would look if every person who owned a business, had children, were married, owed a debt, etc. made sure they had adequate life insurance? Very few people are excited to even discuss life insurance because it can be viewed as a morbid conversation, but we have to change that. For those of us who are in Christ, we shouldn't view death as this horrific event, but rather the time where we receive our eternal reward from God. If we truly keep an eternal perspective, then preparing for the end should be welcomed rather than avoided. No matter where you are financially, risk management helps lay a solid foundation to wealth management. We have financial goals that we want to achieve, but we must make sure that we put something in place in case we don't make it to our intended destination.

Imagine the scenario where a parent ensures that, no matter what happens to them, not only will their loved ones be able to pay off their family home (which historically has been one of the major ways generational wealth has been passed along), but provisions were made for the surviving spouse for income. Also, within the same scenario, any children affected by this death would also have money to pay for college. Picture the business owner who makes plans that, upon their death, their business interest either passes directly to a relative, or money is provided to buy their interest out and their family receives cash payment for what their business is worth. Envision a generation that never experiences being left behind with sorrow and bills. How strong would the body of Christ be, knowing that every family, not only made provisions for each other, but they likely made provisions for their local church, which also impacts the local community?

King Solomon built the temple, largely because his father David had already gathered the resources. There may be things God has laid on your heart to start, but what if it were up to your kids or family to complete the vision or desire that God first gave you? Do you think we would make different decisions if that were the case?

When we look at our communities and churches, especially in cities like Detroit where the average median income is half that of the national average, having adequate life insurance becomes a greater need. It's something that takes great sacrifice because you personally may not benefit from life insurance, but it takes forward thinking knowing that you'll be giving the next generation a better opportunity. I know of families who have continued to not just survive but thrive because they've done the basics of buying life insurance.

Life insurance should really be viewed as a basic necessity, as we view things like a car, house, and health insurance. The common element of any type of insurance is "what if." What are the chances of something happening? This is one of the major factors in deciding the costs of certain insurances. When we look at car insurance, the "what ifs are things like accidents, thefts, vandalism, etc. In health insurance the "what ifs" are the need for care, for sickness, ailments, accidents, normal check-ups, and child births. What about life insurance?

We all know we're going to die. The probability of that event happening is 100%. We must think about the possibility that if that were to happen tomorrow, where would that leave our families? This question is one that needs to be answered by a life insurance professional, but it's one that you should be able to answer right away based on where you are today.

If you were to die tomorrow, would your family be able to continue to pay your mortgage? If so, how long? Could the mortgage be paid off? If there's a family business, would the business be able to continue? Would there be a financial struggle? Would the home be lost to creditors, car repossessed? Would your family just add on to what they already have and be in an even better position for generations to come?

Improper Titling of Assets

All the "wealth killers" are by-products of not following many of the steps that have been laid out in this book. Some of these items are just a matter of not knowing, but some things are a matter of us knowing better and just not doing better.

Improper titling of assets can be a direct by-product of not having, or not updating an estate plan. Remember, your estate plan is not just about when you die, but making provisions if you become ill, incapacitated or when something happens to one of your heirs. This is one of the most common asset titling mistakes. Again, the biggest misconception regarding estate planning is that it's only for the wealthy, and that's just not true. Estate planning is for anyone who has possessions. Another misconception is that estate planning isn't necessary because, "I have beneficiaries on all of my accounts."

Let's look at two quick scenarios. Assume you opened an investment account prior to you being married and at the time you named one of your siblings; but after you married, you forgot to update your beneficiary? If you died those funds would unfortunately go to your sibling. Even if your sibling wanted to give the assets to your surviving spouse, tax laws may not allow that to happen.

Let's now say that you're a senior and you have two children who are your sole living beneficiaries. You name one of your children as joint owner of your checking account to make sure your bills are paid just in case you can't make it to the bank. Though your intentions may be for your children to split everything you have 50/50, if you were to die with one of your children named as a co-owner of your account, technically that money now 100% belongs to the account co-owner. Some siblings have worked it out on their own, and other disputes have ended up pretty ugly. Even if there's no in-family fighting, not having the proper titling on your assets could just send your heirs to probate court, which is a place no one wants to go. Things may have to go through probate if there's no beneficiary listed, or the beneficiaries listed have died.

Having an estate plan and making sure it's reviewed every few years and anytime life events happen, such as a death, divorce, business change or birth, can help ensure that your assets are always properly titled.

Early Withdrawals from Retirement Accounts

There are always exceptions to every rule, but typically taxes and/or penalties come into the picture when money is withdrawn from retirement accounts and retirement type of investments like annuities before you turn 59 ½. Unexpected things do happen, but there are steps that can be taken ahead of time to prevent these early withdrawals.

All of these wealth killers are the result of one or more bricks or stones missing from the building blocks of biblical wealth management. Early withdrawals are often a direct result of a missing budget, savings plan, and accountability. Your retirement account may be the biggest asset you have, so withdrawing from your retirement account could be equally easy and tempting. For one, if you're still working, taking loans from your retirement account is very easy and the interest rate you pay is often lower than a personal loan. Plus, you can avoid taxes and penalties if you pay it back. This is certainly not an endorsement, but just stating how and why people do it. Oftentimes, people don't want to do this, but they feel it is the only thing they can do.

Now, I don't mean those who have had medical issues and must deal with the pile of bills. I'm referring to those who have credit card bills, loans, and either property and/or income taxes. There's usually a pattern as to why the money must be withdrawn and where [401(K), IRA]. The reason is often the fact that many people are 401(K) poor.

Imagine someone who lives paycheck to paycheck, may have a couple hundred dollars in a savings account, and has $100,000 plus in their retirement account. The savings for retirement is great, but this person may not have done as good of a job saving outside of their 401K. When an emergency happens, they will have to use credit, if it's available, and as these emergency financial shortages keep happening, the total grows to the point where it gets out of hand. Once the amount gets to this point, this person decides "enough is enough." They want to get rid of the weight of debt and ultimately decide to withdraw or borrow the funds from their retirement account.

This scenario could be avoided if there was a budget and savings plan in place that required a consistent amount of money be placed in the bank for emergencies and future goals. Let's be honest: Many of us would have no money in our retirement accounts if the plans weren't automated and didn't come out of our check before we're paid. If our 401(K) required us to take the money from our checking account and put it into their plan ourselves, we might be in trouble. We often lack that type of discipline and it's too tempting to spend it on something else. This is why you want to automate your financial life as much as possible.

Most banks and credit unions allow their customers to automatically move money from their checking to savings account, and if you aren't already doing it, I strongly urge you to start doing this. Even better, arrange with payroll to deposit your money where you need it. Many employers allow you to send money to multiple places, so instead of sending 100% of your after-tax paycheck to your checking account, maybe send 98% of your checking and 2% to your savings. If you can afford to do more, by all means do it.

No matter the reason you may find yourself taking early withdrawals, many times it can be traced back to insufficient savings. Outside of the possible taxes and penalties that may come from early withdrawals, many times the money is never paid back; so, you may find yourself taking 5 or 10 years' worth of savings and spending it all at once, only for the money to be slowly paid back. Not only that, but you may lose the ability to make normal contributions into the plan which only costs you potential growth in the long run. The bottom line is do everything possible to avoid these kinds of nowhere-else-to-go scenarios, unless it's part of your retirement withdrawal strategy that you've carefully considered and crafted with your financial advisor.

Using Hope as a Plan

I pray that by this part of the book, you know that most financial goals are possible, and that biblical wealth building comes from wisdom and diligence.

As Christians, we should have more than just the positive thoughts and energy that the world talks about; but a real genuine hope that's built on Scripture. Biblical hope is not just wishing for something that we desire, like me "wishing" the Cleveland Browns would win a Super Bowl. Rather, it's a confidence that we have based on God's promises. If we follow God's way with our finances, He will deliver and allow us to experience what He describes throughout the Bible.

When it comes to finances, the "hope" we often have is completely contrary to what is actually going to help us financially succeed. If you want to retire with some sort of financial stability, you can't just "hope" your way to retirement. It's going to take you working a job or running a business to earn an income, then saving and investing that income and putting it away little by little. If you want to help your children with college, or fund your favorite local charity, you can't just hope that it happens. You must make plans and act on those plans to see those dreams come to life. Many people "hope" to get out of debt, find a new job, or save for retirement, with no true action behind it.

We should absolutely have hope, but hope alone is not going to get us to the finish line. If you want a new job, you need to put in applications, update your resume, and reach out to people. If you want to lose weight, you need to make better dietary choices and start exercising. Whatever you want to see done financially in your life, you can't just "hope" for a pot of gold at the end of the rainbow. Hope is important, but it's not a plan. Make sure whatever you hope happens has some measurable actions to back it up.

Not Trying

The final wealth killer is arguably the most damaging. We're all in different places financially. Some of you reading this may be at your breaking point, but please don't make the mistake of getting so overwhelmed that you quit and don't do anything at all. Remember Galatians 6:9 tells us "let us not grow weary in well-doing, for in due season we will reap a harvest if we don't give up." We don't know when our harvest will come, but if we don't plant the seeds the harvest will never arrive. Though you may be at a breaking point financially, you may also be at a breakthrough, so don't give up on doing things God's way. Be encouraged that God's word, along with Godly counsel and diligence will work. God's plan always works.

Closing Remarks

By now, you may feel overwhelmed. That's not a bad thing. I want you to come to grips with the fact that wealth management is of extreme importance and is a concern of God. Everything you've read is trustworthy because it's in God's Word. It has also been proven through application through the lives of people who are too numerous to count. Please read through this book several times and share it with someone else. The beautiful thing about money is that it's a relative subject for everyone, no matter the financial situation. As I write this, and as you read this, I earnestly pray that you don't just read, but you actually do the work laid out in these pages—allowing you to experience the freedom of following Christ financially!

Throughout this book I've tried to connect the spiritual with the practical, so there are a series of things you can do to get off the hamster wheel that stands in the way of us accumulating wealth. Remember, building wealth is a step by step process, so no matter where you are financially, don't get discouraged. Throughout the Bible, we see God constantly reminded his people to be courageous, to not fear, and that he is with them, and I don't see it any differently as it relates to our finances, but here are a few immediate things you can do today:

- Take inventory of where you are today and where you want to be in the future. This will require some effort, but it's well worth the time you will invest.

- If you recognize that you haven't been the best steward as you could have been, do what we all should do when we recognize we're outside of God's will; repent. This is not to beat you up, but to encourage you to go back to God and ask for greater wisdom and a financial do-over. Remember, the word repent that is found throughout the Gospels and the book of Revelation comes from the Greek word "metanoeō, which means to think differently, or change our mind. To become good stewards of our money, we literally have to change our minds around how we see money. I've had to pray this several times in my life and God has always responded. Remember 1 John 1:9 tells us that if we confess our sins God is faithful and just to forgive us of our sins and cleans us from unrighteousness, so we should go running back to Him

- Create your money system
    - Include a thorough budget either on paper, an Excel spreadsheet, or an app where you're properly recording your income and expenses.
    - Identify needs versus things you want.
    - Commit to living on less, so you can save and invest more.
    - If you take on any payment, whether it be a car note, mortgage, etc, make sure you have the ability to save/invest the same amount of money each month.
    - Automate your savings and investment strategy, so you don't have to think about it, the same way you do your 401K investment.
- Own individual life insurance (not through work) as early as possible, and make sure some of it is permanent to ensure you leave an inheritance to your children's children.
- Protect your ability to earn an income through disability and life insurance planning.

- Don't put off planning for retirement, and make sure your 401K is not the only asset you're investing in for retirement. Consider both ROTH and brokerage accounts.

- Write out very specific financial goals that you want to achieve and set time limits on them. Look at them every day and track them every month.

- Protect your assets through estate planning.

- Find someone to go along this journey with.

- Use this book as a guide or reference point that you can constantly go back to, but seek professionals to help you along the way.

- Get excited about the journey God will take you on.

It's important to remember that God will carry us through all times. God's not necessarily going to dump a bunch of money in our laps, but He's going to give us resources like people and this book to help gain the knowledge we need to come out on the other side. Let's make sure we also never forget what he has already given us, and that's his word through the Bible.

God will always be the best financial advisor you can find. Use the guidance of this book, which is based on the application of God's Word, but his word is the ultimate source. It doesn't mean you won't have difficulties in life, but I'm confident through much reading, prayer, seeking, diligence and application, you will do very well for yourself, your family, your church and, most importantly, the Kingdom of God.

Resource Page

CERTIFIED FINANCIAL PLANNER™ in your area- www.letsmakeaplan.org

Financial Advisor background check - www.brokercheck.com

High yield CD rate and money market rates- www.bankrate.com

Government Bonds - www.treasury.gov

Life insurance and disability insurance need calculator- www.lifehappens.org

Scholarship look-up- www.myscholly.com

ABOUT THE AUTHOR

What many would consider to be a job or career, he considers a calling and a mandate. For Maurice Miller, Jr., money is much more than dollars and cents. As a Certified Financial Planner™, licensed health and life insurance agent, broker, investment advisor, author and entrepreneur, he's not just on a mission to gain greater wealth for himself or his immediate family—he's intentional about helping families and communities as a whole to gain financial wisdom and build long-term wealth He is passionate about providing permanent financial literacy resources to people of all backgrounds, especially those who have not had access to the proper wealth-building tools. Plain and simple, he seeks to give others what his family lacked when he grew up: *access.*

Born to unwed parents, who split by the time he was two or three years old, Maurice realized early on that a big part of the reason they struggled was because they had two incomes, going in two different directions, in two different households. But it wasn't until he attended a predominantly mainstream college that he was exposed to people who took family trips, had family vacation homes, and parents who could pay for college tuition out of pocket. At that point, he knew he had to be missing something. His parents had never had access to a financial advocate or coach, nor the vital tools that create general wealth.

Because he knows firsthand what it's like to lack financial wisdom, Maurice is set apart from the competition. From the onset, he walks clientele through a precise, thorough process. As a financial planner, he doesn't just help them get out of debt or purchase their first home. He positions clients to take a big picture approach by helping them achieve their financial goals in a concise, sensible manner in the most tax-efficient, risk-averse way possible. Educating clientele on the "why" behind every financial decision along the way, he simplifies their complex needs and goals. And while some financial planners and advisors push templates and products, Maurice develops a written strategic plan to justify every decision a customer makes—empowering them to make wise decisions long-term.

An alum of Bowling Green State University, Maurice has spent nearly 20 years in the financial services industry. Three of those years, he served in operations, while he's been a financial planner since 2008. He's spent the last nine years building his independent financial planning practice. He holds a B.S.B.A. in Finance, Series 7 & 66 Securities License, State of Michigan continuing education instructors license for CPA's and other licensed professionals, and the Certified Financial Planner™, Chartered Financial Consultant™, and Certified Exit Planning Advisor™ designations. He has collaborated with a colleague to develop a financial literacy curriculum textbook that any school or homeschooler can use to create a permanent solution for what our modern-day system lacks in the way of financial education. In addition to his book, *When the Word Meets the Wallet: The Financial Bible*, he has also authored a book, *Navigating Your Way To and Through Retirement*.

Maurice has also been recognized as a Five Star Wealth manager for several years, was named in Investment News 2022 40 under 40 for advisors changing the financial services industry, served on the national CERTIFIED FINANCIAL PLANNER™ Disciplinary & Ethics Commission and serviced as the National Chair in 2022, and was inducted into the John Hay High School (Cleveland, OH) hall of fame in 2023.

Maurice has been joyfully married to the love of his life Laneetra since 2012, and they have five children they adore.
To connect with Maurice, visit him at www.millerswmg.com

www.ingramcontent.com/pod-product-compliance
Lightning Source LLC
Chambersburg PA
CBHW030106170426
43198CB00009B/516